MW01097173

COMMON SENSE

The Art of Making Better Decisions

Michael Goodyear

Copyright © 2014 Michael Goodyear

All rights reserved

This book or any portion thereof may not be reproduced or used in any manner whatsoever without the express written permission of the publisher except for the use of brief quotations in a book review.

The author of this book does not dispense medical advice or prescribe the use of any technique as a form of treatment for physical, emotional, or medical problems without the advice of a physician, either directly or indirectly. The intent of the author is only to offer information of a general nature to help you in your quest for emotional physical and spiritual well-being. In the event you use any of the information in this book for yourself, the author and the publisher assume no responsibility for your actions.

ISBN: 978-1-7360892-0-0

Cover design by: Isaac Bravo
Printed in the United States of America
First Printing, 2014

This book is dedicated to all the children that are growing up without enough parental guidance and the loving attention that they so desperately need. This is my way to help you find what you need in life even if you have to do it mostly alone like I did. I'm giving you the cheat codes that I did not have. Use them wisely and change your life. Best wishes and I love you all.

CONTENTS

WHAT THIS BOOK CAN DO FOR YOU

What will increasing your level of Common Sense do for you and how can it help you daily? It is the gift that keeps on giving for the rest of your life. Literally, it will always be there for you if you don't get irrational or overly emotional and not remember to use it.

It helps you to learn how to see opportunities sooner. You become aware of problems before they get too big so you can come up with better and faster ideas to deal with them that benefit *you* the most.

It helps you to learn why to focus most of your energy on the solution instead of dwelling on the problem. You learn to see just *who* your real friends are and ways to deal with what you find.

Common Sense helps you to see that the end result is almost always your decision. It can help you see when to end a relationship, look for another job or change the direction of your life. It helps you make that hard decision to sever all ties with a situation and when you may not want to or need to completely burn that bridge behind you.

Increased common sense is priceless as it gives you more control over the outcome of your interactions with others. It helps you to see if you are keeping pace with the changes in your life.

Just remember, sometimes we move forward, sometimes we stand still or regroup and rest and sometimes we even end up going backwards. It is all part of the process. Winning and failure go hand-in-hand as without both you won't know how to appreciate the other. They both teach valuable lessons. Just remember, change is inevitable regardless of which way it goes. You are steering the ship so you get to make the decisions on the direction you want your life to go *most* of the time.

Do you want more ways to look at the situations that are happening around you? Learning how to develop your own version of common sense can help. Remember, common sense is not common. Many things that happen in life are not common and sometimes they don't really make much sense at all. We can't change the past even if it just happened but learning more common sense can help us to make better choices for the future.

Your confidence level goes up as you take more control over your emotional responses. It helps you to see when to just keep your opinion to yourself and when to stop an argument with someone that you know will never see your point, sometime before it even starts. It helps you to find reasons to walk away and distance yourself from that negative energy.

You can apply common sense to all areas of your life. Increasing your common sense improves your control over the outcome of your decisions.

As you increase your ability to grasp more concepts of common sense and human relations, you will find better ways to use them to deal with many of the stressful situations that come up in your life. It will help to increase your ability to have better human relations with everyone around you because you will recognize many of the things that used to trigger negative responses from you. You will be able to let many of those negative feelings slide by without having negative responses to them in the first place.

How can it help you? If you understand the things that usually trigger bad reactions from you, then you can actually create better control over the choices you make to deal with those things in the future. Life is a series of choices and sometimes we need to take more time to make those choices *if* life allows us that luxury. Just don't stand in the middle of a cross walk to answer a text from someone. Wait until you are on the sidewalk, LOL.

If you don't react negatively to most of the things that come up in your life, then you will be able to calmly deal with them no matter what they are. You just have to understand that everything in life is a lesson and the sooner you learn this lesson the sooner you can move on to the next lesson.

Common sense is simply the art of making the best out of what happens to you in all areas of your life. As humans we sometimes slip up from a life of social conditioning but if we have a working knowledge of common sense and human relations to fall back on then we can move forward quickly with minimal setbacks. It will help you to alter any previous social conditioning that you may have experienced and give you the tools to change that mindset to your benefit.

This book helps you to use your own mind to develop more common sense that will work for you and your life situations. Just remember, even the common sense that works for you today might need some changes for tomorrow situations.

Free advice is worth exactly what you paid for it, absolutely nothing. However if it can help you make better decisions then it becomes useful. You are responsible for the actions that you take and the choices that you make. Common sense just helps you see more choices to pick from so that you can make decisions that you will be happy with and that will work for you in your life situations.

This is a good place to remember Murphy's Law. Almost everything takes longer than you expected, almost everything is usually harder than it seems and if it can go wrong sometimes it will.

Good luck and be careful out there. I wish you peace of mind, love of life and as much happiness as you can create. Remember, we are responsible for our own happiness and we should hold our self accountable for our actions as well. Now go live your best life and do your best to have some fun along the way. My love and prayers to all of you.

ABOUT THE COVER

The cover art is something that portrays my dream of World Peace through learning the wisdom of Mother Nature and applying it to the way we treat the precious life giving planet that she is allowing us to share. Added to that is the love that all humans need to find for each other through mutual respect for our different cultures and finding a way to live and let live and putting an end to greed and war. Then add the Common Sense that needs to be applied to take that love and help repair the very planet that gives us life. This can happen as we find better ways to teach our children about life, love, respect, honesty and better human relations. There is a lot more but this is a good start.

Mother Nature is the main focus as she was here way before we were and will be here long after we are gone. The only way we can extend the time that humans will be here is to learn to be better custodians of this planet and be more understanding of our differences.

The globe is a series of symbolisms that speak of the many things that can help to bring this about. A larger picture of the globe is on the back cover. On the final pages of the book is a description of the symbols I am using, but see if you can figure out what I am saying before you look inside.

I was fortunate enough for my friend Anthony Scolaro and his wonderful design team at *projectassistant.org* to pull my thoughts together into a very organic scene to create the cover art. My biggest heartfelt thanks go out to the entire team.

This book is a social experiment in several ways.

First it is not professionally edited, (I could not afford it). It is not word perfect nor is it professionally formatted.

If you can get past that, there may be something here to learn. We don't demand these things of the music we love or the movies that we watch, so maybe we could tolerate them in order to hear what other humans, without the resources to pay for perfection, have to say. JMHO.

Next, the target audience is young children and others that need "basic" *Common Sense* and better ways to navigate daily life with less stress and anxiety. With all that is going on in the world today, the time to increase that awareness is now. This information would be beneficial to those individuals even if it was in street slang. Again this is just my JMHO.

I hope that my thoughts will help you to see many areas of your life in a different manner so that you may walk through this life with a clearer mind and enough mental skills to be able to bypass much of the BS and human drama that is thrown before you.

If this succeeds it will help to open the door for others to share their thoughts easier. While I realize that the "perfect" book is preferred, I must ask; will you take a chance to hear the message before you judge the messenger? Thank you and enjoy your reading journey with me.

INTRODUCTION

Consider the information in this book to be *Common Sense* 101 as it gets *way* deeper than this. This is written at a level that even preteen children will understand. It will help anyone that wants more ways to look at different areas of *Common Sense*. It also speaks of basic human relations and will show people many different ways that people interact.

Common Sense just needs to be taught to the children by well meaning parents and adults until they can pick it up on their own. Start slow as they can only absorb so much at one time. Every child will pick it up at a different pace and there is no rush as long as consistency is applied.

Remember that the *Common Sense* that will work for you and your children will be different than what works for others. Very few humans' lives are common and many things that happen in life make absolutely no sense. These are just bullet points to help you think before you react. I think of these things as knowledge that I wish someone had shared with me as a child.

You only want to use this to help you create your own thoughts that will help you in your own life situations. These are just my thoughts to help you see more solutions to the situations you encounter every day. You will not get it all perfect, you are not supposed to. Failure is a lesson all by itself. Learn from it.

This is meant to help children at a very early age. Imagine what our lives could be like if the first things we were taught in life was *Common Sense* and human relations. Mix that in with confidence, physical fitness, good eating habits, honesty, and good manners and in the home and by the people we trust the most at that age, our parents. Add to that, love, honor, respect, humility, forgiveness for yourselves and others and we'd have the basic needs met to give us a good start in life, all starting before beginning school. Can you imagine the difference we would see in our children, I can see it as clear as day. If we humans are capable of this then the place where world peace will come from is enlightened children with similar qualities.

Greed, war, hatred, cruelty, and other negative aspects of our current human nature have been bred into the human race since the beginning of it. An efficient way we can change that is to breed a smarter generation that has most of the opposite traits.

It is a great starting point for children to learn these things. It's also a good adding point for older humans, if you want or need it, and you have little or no *Common Sense* yet. I say *yet* because the main point of this book is to get more humans started using more *Common Sense* thinking on a regular and hopefully permanent basis.

Common Sense and human relations needs to be taught to the children at the earliest ages possible, as soon as they learn to walk and talk and at a pace they can handle. I realize there is subject matter in this book that is well above the everyday needs of a 4 to 5 year old but they will grow up quickly and need to already know how to deal with these things before they need to use them. This way, as soon as they can read on their own they can take *Common Sense* and start to use the information, in a manner that works for them, as they grow into it.

Keep in mind that I am just another messenger and if you connect with any of what I am saying then you might want to pick up the message and *adapt* it to work for *you* in *your* life. Try it in *your* life situations and in a manner that *you* think it will work best for *you*.

Like the carpenter says; measure twice, cut once. In other words think at least twice about what you want to do or say and the possible outcome of your actions before acting on them. If there is time and the opportunity then think more times about it if possible. The power of rethinking a thought before it is acted upon is so under appreciated by many people. So this is a good place to remember Murphy's Law; "Everything takes longer than it seems, nothing is as easy as it looks and if it can go wrong, it will!"

This is also a good place to share an Einstein quote: "I think 99 times and find nothing. I stop thinking, swim in silence, and the truth comes to me."

The spacing between the paragraphs is two-fold. First it is to give the reader a moment to pause to reflect on how they might adapt the thought and make it useful for themselves in a way that works with their circumstances. The second is to give them the opportunity to write their own version or notes in the space between the paragraphs thus creating their *own book* of *Common Sense.*

The most basic concept of life is that it keeps changing and we must keep changing with it to grow in a direction that benefits us. That being said, remember that the people and situations around you are constantly changing as well and the *Common Sense* you used yesterday might need to be adjusted to work today. You will be reminded of this all through your reading journey with me. I hope you enjoy it.

If you have no real *Common Sense* yet it helps greatly to view aspects of it in a variety of areas of your life. Look at it in the most basic forms to be able to see it more clearly as you practice it and need it. Then you can start to change the way you deal with your own life situations and the people around you. This can help you to have less stress and better outcomes for your efforts.

Most humans can hear the same thing from several different people yet only really understand it after hearing it from the way only one of them presents it. I will give you a personal example. My first Algebra teacher was an older lady and I did not really connect with the way she taught and I failed her class. The next year I took Algebra again by a much younger man that I did connect with. He used a different approach to teaching and I passed with a B average. Everyone hears the same message better from someone that they connect with. Here's hoping that you connect with my words as I speak about the potential use of *Common Sense* in a variety of situations. Remember to look for what works best for you in your situations.

Speaking of school, learning anything takes practice and repetition. In school subjects are presented in many different ways to reinforce what is being said. This includes *Common Sense*, so things will be presented in slightly different wording in this book with the hopes that you will connect with one of the versions and help you understand the point that is being made here.

The intention of this book is for you to be able to see your own life situations more clearly than you see them now. This can help you to make better decisions before you take action on them so that you can truly enjoy the human experience. These words come from a lifetime of making mistakes and having to go back and fix what I did not have the knowledge or *Common Sense* to do right the first time.

These things have helped me, so only use this information if you feel like it will help you, and test it out by running your own version of it through your mind several times, before you apply it. Remember, this is *life* and anything can work or fail. Be prepared for either outcome.

I hope this information can help you avoid a lot of negative efforts. For what it's worth, I'm 68 and still making my share of mistakes so remember, the lessons never stop and life is always changing. The *Common Sense* that works for you now will change regularly as you get older so be ready and willing to change with it.

This book is also for anyone that grew up without enough parental guidance like I did. My father left when I was around 4 years old and I never saw him again. Mom had to work 2 jobs a day and we had to live in the children's home while I was in the 1st, 2nd and 3rd grade until Mom could get a house for us. It truly was a challenge to start life out that way.

We also moved a lot and I went to 3 different grammar schools, 2 different Jr. High schools and 2 different Sr. high schools. I never got to make long term friends growing up. I did not get to grow up in one house or one neighborhood. I was always the new guy having to start over making new friends and learning new areas.

If you have both of your parents and a permanent home then you are way ahead of many of the rest of us. Please cherish your situation and help out all that you can to make it the best for all concerned. Life doesn't go perfect for many folks so take what you have and do the best you can with it. You will get further ahead and faster if you try to be your best every day that you can. Show your love daily.

This book can help those that grew up in a single parent or no parent household or anywhere that there wasn't much mentorship and guidance towards how to live a full life. It is also for those of any age that are living with the need to see many things from multiple angles. It may help you to see situations from a different perspective other than your own for the purpose of comparison.

You will never know "when" you may need any of this information but knowing about it in advance makes it more familiar when the need arises.

This is not advice that you should blindly follow as these are only my current thoughts. I wish they had been shared with me when I was very young so I could have seen a bigger picture of life at an earlier age. These thoughts help to guide me most of the time and they are constantly changing as I learn better ways of thinking and living. My life continues to change and I must change with it as that is the way it is meant to be. I hope that you can use my words to align your own thoughts with the circumstances in your life in order to create the improvement that you desire. This is only a starting point for you and it will always be changing, just as your life keeps changing, the way you deal with your life will keep changing as well. Remember to always show and speak gratitude for everything that you have been given. Never take anything for granted. A big hug and a thank you to the people that help you will go a long way.

These are most of the things that I wish someone had started explaining to me from the time I started to walk and talk. Think about that. If someone had explained to you, as you were growing up, a lot of the things that you would experience in life and a variety of *Common Sense* ways to deal with them then you might have had less negative experiences. They could have been *AHA* moments and you would have just kept moving forward without all the questions, arguments, drama, stress and confusion.

This is also for those that were left alone too much, abused or basically fending for themselves all or most of their life and those that are living that life right now. Those of us that heard all too often; children are to be seen and not heard. Then there is the phrase that they used to motivate you: when you asked them a question they would say; that is for me to know and for you to find out. My thoughts were, really, could you at least point me in the right direction? A good reply to them would be; will you please share your knowledge of it with me?

Those circumstances make learning or hearing, good, intelligent, thought provoking advice almost non-existent. With little or no guidance, almost everything has to be learned the hard way, usually repeatedly, and not always with the best outcome. You basically just react to your circumstances and hope that what you do works and that you don't get hurt doing it. This is my attempt to share a version of *Common Sense* that I hope gives those people a better head start. There are also thoughts in here that can help many people of all ages. It's just another view of the world through a different set of eyes and even my views are changing as my life does, so will yours.

One of the best ways to prosper physically and mentally is to change the way you deal with problems that arise in your life. Most people focus only on the problem itself, they talk about it and relive it by telling others that they know what is wrong and what happened. They wonder how it could have happened to them, how they might have avoided it, and even how they can keep from having it happen again. While understanding these things is essential, to learn why it happened, don't focus on them too long. There is a better approach.

If you have a problem, do not focus or fixate on the *problem.* Focus on the *solution.* The *solution* has the best chance to fix the *problem.* The only thing that focusing on the problem does is make it bigger with all the energy you are focusing into the problem itself. Why not use all of your energy towards finding the *solution.*

One way to do that is to look at others who have solved the same or a similar problem. Then ask yourself; how you might use some of those ideas to help solve your own problem. You can also ask for help or advice. Just remember, free advice is worth exactly what you paid for it, absolutely nothing. Yet, if it can help, by all means try it. Just be ready to adjust if needed and always think things through before you act on them.

One of the best ways towards a solution is to think about "how" you feel about what happened. Then ask yourself just "what" would make you feel better. As long as it is not revenge, as that is a negative emotion that will keep you focused on your problem. Think about a solution that would make you feel better about what happened. Then focus on those good feeling thoughts and keep moving forward and always stay flexible with the solution that you are considering.

Just remember, not all problems have a complete solution. Some problems must just be learned from and let them go and move forward with your life. They just aren't worth the time to continue to deal with them. They are like a relationship where two people have grown apart, just learn from it, let go of it and move on.

This brings us to limiting beliefs. Let's say that you thought the world was flat and you believed that until you saw a picture of the Earth, taken from space, and saw that it was round. You would discard the flat earth belief. Or what if you believed you can't do something or can't live without something or someone? Then something happens to that person or the thing you thought you couldn't live without or the relationship that was so special goes separate ways. Now you are forced to make that change.

Now you see that you can endure those situations and maybe even thrive and do better. Or you at least learn something from the experience. Then you see that your old beliefs about those things were only holding you back from the better life that the universe had waiting for you all along and that thing that was taken away was the Universe's way of getting you where you needed to be sooner.

There are many times in life that we will find that we start believing in things that turn out *NOT* to be true or they just don't work for us anymore. If we are smart we will change our beliefs sooner and move on.

This is a good place to throw in a story by an unknown author to give you an example of what I am saying.

Once upon a time there was an old farmer who had worked

his crops for many years. One day his horse ran away. Upon hearing the news, his neighbors came to visit. "Such bad luck," they said sympathetically.
"Maybe," the farmer replied.

The next morning the horse returned, bringing with it three other wild horses. "How wonderful," the neighbors exclaimed.
"Maybe," replied the old man.

The following day, his son tried to ride one of the untamed horses, was thrown, and broke his leg. The neighbors again came to offer their sympathy on his misfortune.
"Maybe," answered the farmer.

The day after, military officials came to the village to draft young men into the army. Seeing that the son's leg was broken, they passed him by. The neighbors congratulated the farmer on how well things had turned out.
"Maybe," said the farmer.

--Zen Parable

The point here is that things are not always what they seem to be at first glance. So don't over react when something happens. Sit back and watch to see how the next series of events starts to unfold. Most things happen for a reason so step back and look for that reason and if you don't see a reason at least learn from what happened.

This is a natural part of growing older and seeing the changes in our lives. Embrace the change, let go of the limiting beliefs and grow from the experience. Holding onto any of them will only hold you back from growing in the direction that your life is taking you. Like now, even though I am still editing this introduction, this paragraph is screaming at me to get this book published soon.

Limiting beliefs are kind of like an old dead worn out car, if it will cost you more money, stress and time than it is worth to fix it then just call the scrap yard and make a few bucks off of it and let it go. Just go find your next car. That is unless it is a classic of course and you truly want to fix it.

As I have grown older I find that I am quite interested in what works and what doesn't. I watch the things that other people try to do, their reasons and intentions for doing them and then the way that their situations actually turned out.

I look at my own failed projects and the ones that worked, as well as those of the people around me, on the news, and the internet as well. Almost every time, the end results are determined by whether the planning was good and well thought out or not. Even though some of the well thought out plans failed too, there were just less of them that failed. The weird thing is that some things actually work out with basically no planning at all. I guess that proves there is luck!

This is where *Common Sense* should come in and show us the

way. The problem is that we are not born with *Common Sense*. It doesn't come naturally, usually has to be learned the hard way and is rarely taught in school or at home. This is why we should share our knowledge with those that ask for it. It needs to be taught to our children early. In my opinion, "Knowledge not shared is lost and wasted". That's why we still don't really understand how they built the pyramids. That knowledge was either, lost, destroyed or hidden instead of being shared and handed down.

I am by no means an expert on this subject. I am willing to look at *Common Sense* from a wide variety of areas where it could help the average person to have consistently better outcomes by using it before they move forward into projects and life situations. This is the method that I try to use in my own life. It's not perfect but it helps.

I'm not saying that this version of *Common Sense* will work for everyone, or anyone except me. Maybe not even myself in some situations or at different times. I hope it will help you see many other ways to approach different subjects in your life with an open mind before doing something that is not well thought out.

If you have nowhere else to start, just use this book and evolve from where you are in your own or your family's situation and move forward. It's easy to take one idea and *adapt* it to be useful in another situation especially if you have enough different subjects to choose from. That is why I try to show many different areas of life where *Common Sense* can be used. Above all be flexible and ready to adjust if your first thoughts aren't working or you see an even better way to deal with your situation.

It was suggested to me by someone that I was talking to about these things to write a book about it, so I did, and if it only helps one more person then it will have been worth it. This book is simply one of many ways to look at things from one of many *Common Sense* perspectives.

Common Sense (IMHO) is the concept of; am I doing the best thing for myself, most of the people around me and the Earth and will it really help and work out? Ask yourself: what is the best thing to do for the situation at hand and how it might benefit yourself and the most people in your life. The feelings of "all" of the people around you should only be of concern if you will physically hurt any of them. You cannot shape your life worrying about what "everyone" around you thinks. All of them will have a different opinion. We shape our lives by the thoughts that we think, the actions that we take, the way we take care of our bodies, minds and our spirits. Stay as happy, healthy and as in the present that you can and always live with love in your heart.

One more thought on *Common Sense* and the other topics in this book and the sharing of these ideas. I have had wonderful conversations with like-minded folks (family, friends and complete strangers) about all of these subjects. I have also had arguments with other similar individuals who don't really think much about these *Common Sense* ideas. It seems that as long as their life, their health and their current relationships are currently working for them that is all that counts whether it makes sense or not. That is their choice and you must allow them to have it.

Some will even argue against some *Common Sense* subjects but this is true of all subjects. There is always someone that will argue for or against almost anything. Be ready and willing to drop any subject if an argument begins and it will help to keep stress out of your life to drop it. You just won't see eye to eye with everyone on everything so learn to change the subject in a timely manner if your conversation starts an argument that you don't want to participate in. Unless, you feel the need to defend your opinion and even then you must ask yourself; is it truly worth the effort? Does the other person even care?

Another option, other than changing the subject, is to look at the clock and act like you have an appointment somewhere else or need to be somewhere else soon and excuse yourself and leave which will end the argument as well. There are some people that won't stop arguing until you are gone. If a discussion turns into an argument it is rare that it will be beneficial to either of you, mainly because our egos sometimes refuse to back down even if we are wrong.

Some people only become interested in these subjects when their health starts to fail them (like the smoker that refuses to quit until they have a heart attack). Some folks wait until something they are doing (like running red lights until they get caught or have a wreck) or a relationship they are having falls apart from a lack of *Common Sense* (like the person cheating on their significant other and finally gets caught). That is when they will finally care to speak about these things. Until that point most humans usually deny there is even a problem. You must move past denial and accept that there is a problem to fix anything.

So, if you find these subjects worthy of conversation and go to share them with family, friends, or strangers, beware that if they show no interest then you need to stop talking about it and change the subject. If they have no interest then you cannot even have a good discussion about it with them. It will just turn into an argument and it is not the point of this book or *Common Sense* to start a fruitless argument.

This is one of a few reasons that this book has taken 5 years to get ready to publish. There were also health issues, writers and editors blocks as well as work and family issues. Some folks, very close to me, naysayers that made me cast doubt on my own thoughts to the point of wondering if this book is worthy of the readers time. However even that had a reason as it made me look deeper into my own words and refine them and take anything out of the original work that did not have good reason to be in the book. It also gave me time to add more thoughts along the way.

I am finally at the point where I will let the readers decide for themselves what to think of it. That being said if you find these thoughts to be less than you want or need in your life, I bet you know someone around you that can benefit from this book.

Please pass it on to them but only if they truly want it.

Like all books it will only be truly appreciated by like-minded people that want or need a change in their life. I hope that you are one of them. Thank you for taking the time to purchase this book and read my thoughts.

Common Sense cannot fix what has happened to you in the past but I hope that the thoughts in this book will show you how to unwind your feelings about your past. It can help you to examine it for what it was, make some kind of sense out of it and start the process of making peace with it because you can't change it. It made you who you are at this moment. From there you can make plans to heal from it if necessary, learn from it and guide your future in a manner that benefits you. Mentally healing from your past is essential to creating the future you wish to enjoy and fall in love with.

I know that you can do this as we all can with practice, patience, determination and constant focus. You can also become whoever you want to and go wherever you desire within reason. Remember to respect others as much as they deserve it and always respect yourself with your thoughts, words and your actions.

No matter where you are in life, remember that you are loved even if you don't feel it at the time. You have the power to make your life whatever you want it to be, so be patient with yourself as you have a lifetime to get there. Actually you are not trying to get "*there*" it is the *journey* that you are here to enjoy.

Remember that if your God woke you up another day then he did his job. The rest of the day is up to you. So you have to be ready when your opportunity knocks. You have to actually get up and answer the door before it moves on to somebody else. There are new opportunities every day so go explore them.

If you find that this book of Common Sense has helped you or enlightened you to better ways to look at the things happening in your life then please drop by my Face Book page www.facebook.com/readcommonsense. Twitter page, https://twitter.com/readcommonsense and share your thoughts with me and others.

Signed,

A Concerned Human Being

CHAPTER 1
TO THE CHILDREN

To the children first; because you are the future and you are very important. The problem is that the age which the children must be reached and start the teaching of *Common Sense*, Human Relations, Love, Honor, Respect, Intelligence, Courage, Integrity, Faith, Knowledge and Understanding is as soon as they are able to start to speak. That is the beginning of the intellectual connection with them. This can be started while we are teaching them the basics such as how to feed themselves, exercise, read, think, cleanliness and basic survival. Then just give them all the love you can so they will trust and believe that what you teach them is true.

So it is up to you, the parent or any family member or friend to teach the children as early as possible with that truth. As a parent, grandparent, family member or friend, your place in the new child's life is very important and needs to be taken very seriously if the child is to be all he or she is capable of becoming.

Your place is to love, support, teach and show the child the many ways that humans interact and connect. This way they will be able to not just survive being here but to thrive and learn how to duck, slide and weave around most of the obstacles of life when dealing with other humans. You must also teach them when to stand up and speak the truth and defend it and how to be fair with everyone as much as possible. Also teach them when to just shut up and walk away when necessary. Many times this will be realized after the fact so remember it when it happens so as not to repeat it any more than it has to be.

You must reach them with this information before you get them a cell phone (hold off on the phone as long as possible) or they will be too preoccupied with it to pay attention to you. This also means that you must not ignore them while you are playing around on your phone. You must reach them before they begin to interact with other humans in public settings whose families have not figured this out yet. This way they will know not to behave in irresponsible ways but to tolerate those that have not been taught as well. Teach them to share their knowledge with those that will listen and those who enjoy having intelligent conversation but to change the subject or walk away if others show no interest.

If you think that these concepts sound too far ahead of young children to comprehend then you will be surprised by the ones you actually reach as they grasp the concept. Remember, they can figure out a cell phone at this age! If they are exposed to these topics instead of mindless video games and even more mindless TV shows they will progress quickly.

Each generation has the chance to alter the direction of life on this planet. This will happen from the concepts they are taught growing up. Be very open and honest with them so they learn how to make good choices.

Chose your thoughts and the directions that you choose to go wisely. Not all of our thoughts are meant to be acted on immediately and some not at all. Some thoughts come earlier than needed to teach you what to do in a future situation and some come too late but teach what to do the next time the same thing happens.

One of the first things that all humans need to be taught is how others come and go in our lives. We meet most new folks with a smile and a hello and then get to know them and begin to interact with them. Then we either allow them to share more time in our life or move on.

We need to learn to let them walk out of our life experience just as easily. It sounds way easier than it is but we can eliminate a lot of heart ache by doing so and life will teach you this lesson eventually as it did me, especially with the opposite sex. The question is; how many relationships will it take for you to learn this lesson. Knowing this sooner would have saved me many a heartache.

Humans either grow together or we grow apart. It does not mean that either person is wrong unless one physically or mentally hurts the other. Growing apart seems to occur more often than growing together as some folks come into our lives just to teach us something or show us more about ourselves. If we will just look deep enough into each relationship we will see what we need to learn from it. I will speak more of this throughout the book in different ways for different perspectives on it. By the way, I am still learning this one myself because each relationship is different and will show you different things about yourself.

Now to the children that have learned to read. The guides you will have in your life are many and varied: Your parents, family members, teachers, friends, your life experiences, your fears, your thoughts, the things you love or don't love and your own actions, as well as classmates, employers, employees, co-workers, animals, places that you live or visit and many strangers, places and things along the way that will help to guide you through life. "Always look for the lesson in everything that happens in your life" both good and bad. It all happens to teach us more about ourselves. Listen to your life carefully.

Let's break this down, your parents, they love you but they are busy making and keeping a home for you and the family, working, paying the bills, keeping the home clean, cooking and trying to have a personal life as well. Now you may see why they can't spend all of their time with you. If they include you in most things then you are truly a lucky child so be sure to show them your appreciation by being the best person you can be and help-ing out around the house.

That being said, they should make time for their children no matter what. This should be quality time if they are capable of it. Some parents are not able to do this because they lack the know-ledge to be parents in the first place or because of their work schedule such as a military person away from home or a travel-ing business person.

They may not have had good parental guidance themselves or they had children too early in life and do not know yet how to be good parents. They may have conditions (mentally, physically or emotionally) that keep them from being able to perform the role of a parent. There is a lot more to parenting but this will help you understand a lot if you will think about it. However, if you feel that you are being left out or alone too much, by all means speak up politely and ask if they will spend more time with you.

If your parents can't or won't spend time with you then ask a grandparent, an Uncle or Aunt, brother or sister, or simply a good friend to spend that time with you. Good quality love and mentorship comes from many different places. Learn where to look for it and don't hold bad feelings for someone that is not capable of giving you that time and being there for you.

Always cherish the time you spend alone as that is time for you to reflect on how your life is unfolding. Stay as positive as you need to see the lesson in everything because there always is one. Being alone also gives you time to have your own thoughts without distraction.

The places you go and daily circumstances that come up as well as other things that happen will also help you to learn about life. These things all have lessons for you and it is your job to figure out what the lessons are and learn from them and move on to the next lesson. Everything in life is a lesson to be learned and the sooner you figure the current lesson out the sooner you can move to the next lesson.

Your friends will come in many forms, male and females, large and small, many races, many emotional ranges and many ages. If they are good to you and help you and take good care of you then keep them in your life. If they are mean to you or make you do things that you do not want to do or feel like it is wrong for you to do, then ask them to stop being that way or go make better friends. If your parents are physically or mentally mean to you then you may have to ask an Aunt, Uncle or Grandparent if they will take you in. If you have to, just stay out of sight when you can either in another room or outside playing.

Friends will come and go. "Remember to let people walk out of your life as easy as you let them walk into your life". No hard feelings are necessary, just move on. We all change and it doesn't make either person wrong, unless one is hurting the other. People either grow together or they grow apart. It's just that simple. Forgive, forget and let go of all negative experiences. The more positive you stay the better your life will be.

Your life experiences will be varied and many. They will be easy and hard, some will last a long time and some will be short. They will teach you and test your ability to grow from them. How long it takes you to learn from them is up to you. The sooner you see the point trying to be made or the lesson to be learned and make the necessary adjustment in your life, the sooner you will move on to the next lesson. The lessons never stop, just keep moving forward, you will soon understand and it will just become a part of you growing up.

Your fears and your thoughts will come from your life experiences and some will be inherited. Inherited means, what you were taught by your parents, at school, by society, your friends, TV, and the internet. Not all of it will be right for you. What works and is right for your Father, Mother, your family, or your friends might not be right for you so try to learn the difference quickly.

All of these things will change over your lifetime by your experiences, all of them can be right or wrong depending on your circumstances at different times in your life. Never treat any of them as right for you "all" the time because different situations change everything. Life is constantly changing so be ready to keep changing with it.

Do your best to face your fears unless they will harm you to do so. Always question your thoughts because we have both good and bad thoughts. Some of them should be acted upon, others are best forgotten and that applies to both the good and bad thoughts. The best intentions can go either way.

Your life experiences and your fellow travelers can help you figure out which thoughts are right or wrong. Remember, timing is everything and some things will only be right or wrong because of that timing. Farting in the bathroom is normal but at the dinner table at grandma's house it is a whole different situation.

The things that you love and your own actions will change all through your life or at least most of them will, expect it. As you sample all that life has to offer, you will find things that you love and things that you don't. They all have a purpose and a lesson for you if you will look deep enough into them. Once again, learn that lesson and move on.

Keep the things you love in a special place in your heart and visit them often. Remember the things that you don't like now, so you can see if you change your mind about them later in life. Here again, timing is everything.

One thing to remember in life is that when we do anything with others we are co-creating. That is important. Many times we, or someone we know, will have what we or that person believes to be a great idea. While it has potential to be that, it also has potential to fail to be that for some of the others concerned that are expected to be a part of that plan.

When we are co-creating, always remember to allow others to see your idea with no bias and allow them to decide whether or not to join you with no pressure. Most plans work best when everyone wants to be a part of it.

A key question to ask is; since we live as co-creators and we are all responsible for our own happiness. "When is it that the way you decide to make yourself happy means that another human has to be miserable because of it"? Always try to be sure that what you are doing to make yourself happy is not hurting another.

Always ask if what you want to do is something others even care to do or participate in. Never assume that it is. Always be ready to hear "no" and allow others to make their own choice. There are extenuating circumstances to this concerning authority figures which I will discuss later in the book.

Now, take this information with you as well as the information in the rest of the book and only use what works for you at that time and adjust that to fit your needs. As you grow, age and move through life all of this will change. Look for it and be ready to change with it.

It will help you a lot to create the life of your dreams in your own mind now so that it can come to you when the universe sees the

chance to send it your way, be patient. Believe in the power of your thoughts. Close your eyes and imagine the life you want as vividly as you can.

I use affirmations and here are some of mine: I am a creative genius, the Universe supports my every effort, I am free to be my best self at all times, at every turn opportunity appears before me and I see it clearly and act on it accordingly, I can accomplish anything I set my mind on, I deserve love, success and happiness, I have abundant energy, vitality and well-being, I have everything I need right now to accomplish everything I want, my possibilities are endless, I am fit, healthy and attractive, I am worthy of love, I will remain unaffected by negative attitudes around me, my inner vision is always clear and focused, I possess an endless supply of creativity, energy and tolerance for any project that I assume, wealth is pouring into my life, I attract positive people into my life and I am grateful for all of them and I support them as well. Feel free to add any affirmations that you feel will help you grow in the direction you wish to.

I love you all and pray for you to have many wonderful life experiences. Remember, think good thoughts because your thoughts and the words that you speak will create your life, believe in them and give them time to manifest. Now, go have fun being a human being with unlimited potential!

CHAPTER 2
COMMON SENSE:
HOW TO GET MORE
OF IT IN OUR LIVES

If you Google *Common Sense*: first you get, *Common Sense* Media. Second, the dictionary explanation: sound prudent judgment based on a simple perception of the situation or facts. Then, a booklet/pamphlet written by Thomas Paine about the government in 1776 before the beginning of the American Revolution! I do recommend that everybody should read his book. It rings true today as well as it did when he wrote it. I titled this book before I was aware of Thomas Paine's work. As you read, you will see why I chose this title.

You also get many websites and books that talk about *Common Sense* on a single subject or a few as well as people's opinions of it. However, there are very few websites that try to cover the bulk of the basic subject matter, especially for the young people with no real mentors. The sites that come up are varied topics about *Common Sense* and the great self help teachers of our time who I salute. I just feel that we should be trying to help the people who don't even know to look for the great teachers yet. Teach it in the home and in the schools where most of these people are. Doing so could be a light bulb moment for many to see the bigger picture faster.

Growing up, we heard simple things like: "keep your fingers out of car doors", "don't touch the stove when it's red hot or it will burn you", "pick up your toys so nobody trips over them", "don't play in the street", "don't stare at the sun" and many other unique bits of wisdom. We need more than this, as discussed in detail in the rest of the book and at the earliest age possible.

Common Sense is a lifelong continuing educational experience. It never stops, but it's usually taught to us by the school of hard knocks. We seem to learn a lot of it by experiencing it first hand and by our own failed attempts to fix or create things. A large portion of *Common Sense* it seems must be learned in that manner. The rest could be learned much easier by well meaning people freely sharing their knowledge to those around them that they see struggling.

Some people never seem to see what they are doing that is holding them back. So they continue to do the same thing over and over. Maybe with more people setting a good example and sharing that knowledge, even those that are struggling might see an answer sooner and with fewer failed attempts. However, there will always be those that refuse to see things any other way than they are currently using. You will have to cut your losses here and move on and just pray for them to see the better way eventually.

Wouldn't it be nice to be able to eliminate many of our failed efforts, some of our busted knuckles and stubbed toes with an ongoing course in *Common Sense*? Not all of them though, as some struggles seem to be a driving force with mankind. Shouldn't we be teaching our children from an early age a lot of the *Common Sense* ways to possibly deal with life in all areas? How to deal with friends and family in most situations! How to handle money so we can save and have more! How to deal with situations that will come up in public, at school, at work and in other areas of life! Also, that those situations will always be changing and needing different answers to get the best results as they change. *Common Sense* says that we should always be ready to change with new situations as they come up.

I didn't get a human relations course until I went to a technical college after high school. So try this, next time you have a group of 12 or more together send at least 5 of them out in the hall or to another area where they cannot hear what is being said. Tell a short story to the group that is left and send one of them out to get someone from the other group. Have that person relate the story to the person they got out of the hall. Then that person goes and gets another and relates the story. Then have that person repeat what he just heard. By the time it is repeated to the last person it usually changes a lot from the original version. This is what happens in life as well and why you can't count on 2nd hand information being correct.

We should get human relations and *Common Sense* taught to us in the home and the 1st, 7th, 10th and 12th grades in school. Those are the years of big change for kids. It could also be a continuing online blog, forum, or social network of mentors helping others who haven't figured things out yet.

I don't mean actually telling folks what to do as they need to make final decisions based on person preferences. Just give them wise council to help them sort out their own thoughts in a manner that works best for that situation.

This has started to happen in all types of forums, blogs and Twitter etc but only if you look in specific places or follow specific people. Wouldn't it be nice to search for Common Sense and find many sites that deal with most aspects of it?

If Common Sense and human relations were taught to us from childhood on, it would be a more normal thing and we could reduce much of the stress, pain, conflict, worry and confusion that exist today.

Our jails, prisons, hospitals and graveyards are filled with people who failed to use good old *Common Sense*. We can change that.

Put up more *Common Sense* shows to help everyone with life situations and decisions or just start a *Common Sense* channel. Guide your children to the current cartoons that teach it instead of the ones that teach them to be crazy. Tell them the story of the boy that cried wolf too many times or any other teaching fairy tale. Make more shows for teens that help them understand better ways to grow up, how to deal with others. Teach them honesty, respect, integrity, gratitude, appreciation and human relations.

Teach them not to bully anyone and how to walk away and not put up with it if it is happening to them. Or better yet if you see a bully coming go the other way or try to get to a safe place and travel in groups for safety. I know that it is tougher than this in real life but thinking ahead about these things can keep your guard up. Bullies usually try to catch others alone and in private places where they can't be seen or stopped. Tell your children that it is always ok to tell their parents or an authority figure that it is happening. Teach them some type of self defense if you can.

There is a lot of this information out there but parents have to find it and make the time to share it with their children at the earliest age possible so it will stick with them. And by all means tell them *why* these things are preferred or necessary.

The funniest videos shows are full of *Common Sense*, "don't do this clips", but we laugh at them instead of learn from them. Let's teach people to THINK. I mean to think our actions through all the way from start to finish if you have the time. Think your own ideas through your own head many times before acting on them to work the kinks out. Talk about your thoughts with a really trusted friend so that you can get another perspective on it from someone else. Even if they don't understand it or see it the same way, a lot of times it will give you more perspective on it just speaking out loud so you can hear it. Thinking is a process and the first thought is only the beginning of it.

I realize that we can't always apply *Common Sense* to all situations and jobs. Some jobs and some of life's problems just aren't common. Some situations in life make no sense at all. There will always be these situations and jobs. Think them through carefully before acting on them. Sometimes things just happen too fast and we have to do the best we can in the moment. If we have a good education in *Common Sense* from childhood we will possibly make better quick decisions as well.

This discussion of *Common Sense* is for the bulk of the rest of the time when you can use it, if you just take a moment to think your thoughts all the way through to several different outcomes.

Maintain focus on your goal but think about the best possible outcome of each step in the process, a good one, the worst one, the one you didn't expect and most of the things that could possibly go wrong along the way!

If your goal is to get to work on time and your car breaks down or you miss the bus then you call a taxi or a friend. We get married with the best intentions and love for each other but if you find yourselves incompatible it may be wise to go your separate ways before make the relationship worse. If you start a job and find that the work is too demanding of you or that you can't perform your duties without hurting yourself it is also wise to look for work more suited to your abilities. Many other areas in life need anything from minor to major adjustments as you work toward your goals.

So stay ready to make any necessary adjustment, even if that adjustment means just stopping the current plan because it didn't work. That is the key, always be ready to adjust with plan B, or even C, D, E etc. There is seldom any dishonor in failure as it happens to all of us but there are a lot of dead people that failed to be ready to change a plan.

So, will *Common Sense* ever take its proper place in our education system, our homes and in our workplaces? I hope that it will soon. It will be simple to do if it starts as early as possible in the home with family support. Turn off the TV and the cell phones for a little bit each day. Then have discussions about *Common Sense* ways that the family will get along better, more efficiently and create a common goal to help every member get ahead faster. This creates incentive for everyone. If one member feels left out, find out why quickly and resolve that issue.

Learning *Common Sense* needs to start at the earliest age possible when children still look up to and *want* to talk to their parents.

Ideally it should start *before* they start school or get a cell phone and delay that as long as possible. Never let the TV be the baby-sitter unless you have good quality *Common Sense* entertainment or nature, art, music, science and true history shows for them to watch.

Most kids are like little sponges just wanting attention so give

them positive, loving, *Common Sense* attention. Teach them human relations first. If you have no better place to start then use this book as a reference of ideas to choose from, but evolve to what is working best for your family situation and the situations your children are dealing with.

Never tell a child, or anyone, *NO or what to do without telling them* WHY. Take a minute, you are their teacher and they need to have motivation and it is you that can provide that. When they understand *why* they will usually try harder.

If *Common Sense* is taught in the family to the children at the earliest age it will be easier to keep it going in the school system and on through life.

Ignorance is when we don't know something yet. Stupidity is when we know better and do it anyway. With more *Common Sense* we can eliminate a lot of stupidity. The time to teach *Common Sense* to the children is now. I hope this little book will help to plant some of those seeds.

CHAPTER 3
COMMON SENSE:
LET'S USE IT.
IT'S TIME.

This book is not written to be an authority on the subject. It's just meant to be beginner topics that encourage the use of it in areas of life where it could be of help and in general situations to consider other ways to apply it. It can also be used as a starting point for discussions about it in all areas of life. Remember not to tell anyone to do something the way it works for you as their situation is probably different and may need adjustment to make it work for them. That is unless it is a work/boss/employee situation or someone that has no clue where to start.

I'm not a wordsmith and have never written a book before, so this is my attempt to bring my thoughts on *Common Sense* to print. So I am talking and writing about *Common Sense* from my heart and my life experiences and how it has and is helping me. I hope that it at least becomes an added jumping point to all the others speaking about *Common Sense* to help to bring it into the mainstream of life. This is just another way of approaching the subject and it needs to happen soon so why not now?

Some parents are already teaching their children *Common Sense* and I applaud them. Everyone should, so why not start teaching this to all children at an early age, along with respect, honesty, appreciation and integrity for self and others? How can we get it to those that need it most and at the earliest age possible? It needs to start in the *home. Parents, Common Sense is the best gift you can give to your children other than love.*

I live in a rural area that has what seems to be a horrible situation happening all too frequently. I have heard of kindergarteners and elementary school children who will curse a teacher out and throw things at them. Then they are kept in school. Then I read the national news to hear that someone in high school got kicked out of school for saying something that is considered to be religious or for praying. This is backwards and our authorities need to address this.

There needs to be consistency in our school system so these things can be balanced out. Teachers need a button on their desk to call for help and a witness such as cameras in the classroom. Teachers need to know how to protect themselves, as well as know when to not over react. The school needs to back them up and suspend children that act out in unhealthy ways.

If you have children, seek wise counsel to help you teach them. Be a good role model, spend quality time with them. Show them by taking care of yourself, your family and your belongings as well as you can. 1Simply by showing children that you do the right thing will show them how to do the same.

If you have a job, do it the best that you can. No matter what your role is, it doesn't matter if you are doing menial labor or working as a top CEO or politician. If you do it the best that you can, things around you stand a much better chance of changing for the better. Just ask yourself; "Is this for the good of the majority, or the few? Is it right, or is it wrong?" There should be only one truthful answer to most subjects. Occasionally there are grey areas that come up and have to be dealt with in a different manner, handle those situations with caution.

Remember, repeatedly doing the same thing and expecting different results, does not work! Many things that are not working now can be adjusted with a few simple changes to get much better results. Humanity can pull together and fix this mess. We created it and we can reverse it. Many have already started but all people need to chip in and help our world become a better place.

It seems to be a game now, for some, to hurt others just because they can. Surely there are better things to do than playing games that involve hurting others just for the fun of it or just to prove that you can to impress your friends. If these people were taught to not hurt others, in childhood, maybe a lot of this might not be happening now.

Everyone makes mistakes and sometimes bad choices. If *Common Sense* ways were taught in the home as well as at school on a broader scale, we could change some of these bad things that are happening now. This is where sharing your knowledge and mentoring those around you will help tremendously.

Imagine if only one percent more of just the US population, approximately 3,300,000 people, started using more *Common Sense* in all areas of their lives. The snowball effect would be tremendous, and if one percent of the approximately 7.67 billion people of the earth started using more and better *Common Sense*, that would be 767 million people using better *Common Sense*. That alone would go a long way to creating a better world for all and it could be immediate. It has already been at work for a long time, but now more than ever it needs all the help and momentum that it can get.

If you have good *Common Sense*, share it with anyone that will listen. Let me say this again; "**Knowledge not shared is lost and wasted.**"

I encourage everyone to use it more often, think about it, meditate on it and bring it mainstream into the lifeblood of our society and our planet. There is a lot of talk about the lack of *Common Sense*. Shouldn't there be even more talk about using *better Common Sense*?

I am repeating this to make the point that it's time to use more *Common Sense*, what are we waiting for? Let's use *Common Sense* as a common topic of conversation and a way of life. Let it be taught in the home, school, church and all institutions as a full subject matter from 1st grade on. Let there be more discussion boards about it with everyone putting their best thoughts forward. Make more *Common Sense* games, songs, stories and even more movies showing better ways to use it. If we are lucky, it will catch on.

Is there a better time to start than now? Remember, the hardest step is the first one and it gets easier from there.

So, start your own book of *Common Sense*. It's just a daily journal either written or kept mentally to keep you on track. What worked for you and what did not! Who helped and who hurt and why? What made you feel great, and what made you feel bad? What work or play inspired you? Write daily little notes to yourself or make mental notes for future reference. Refer to it often. Keep it close and add to it whether you had a good day or a bad day. You will learn a lot from it and the act of writing it down will help you to remember it. Update your feelings about everything in it regularly, because it will change as your life moves forward. It should help to keep you from making the same mistakes repeatedly. Guard it closely, for it is your insight into *YOU*. It's not for others to judge you by, but they will if they read it. Remember to keep your most personal thoughts to yourself.

CHAPTER 4
RANDOM THOUGHTS

I am only a human asking questions and wondering in statements about what could be if we shifted our focus. Please don't consider any of this as more than my opinion, as every situation is different and so is each person's way to deal with it. I hope that this book will give you more ways to think about things as you deal with what comes up in your life. I don't claim to be an authority on the subject and I know I have not used it as much as I wish I should have in days gone by.

There were times when I should have held my tongue and times when I shouldn't have. Then there times that I made a big deal out of something that I never should have! There were also opportunities that I lost because I didn't trust my instincts and seize the moment, and especially those times that I should have just relaxed and enjoyed the moment. I think all of us have had these moments and if we are lucky then we at least learned from them.

My hope is that asking these questions and pondering these

thoughts might help someone else get further along faster so that it will help speed up their learning curve.

I wish that there had been someone who had asked me these questions, or spoken these thoughts to me, from the time I started to walk and talk. Would I have listened to them? I hope that I would have and if they were my parents or teachers that were showing me love and I could see things working out better because of it I am sure that I would have.

Could I have actually heard them in a way that I would have made useful? Spoken at a very early age by someone that I looked up to for guidance, I can almost certainly say yes, I would have at least heard them. Spoken often enough with that persons own actions being the same to reinforce it I can see where I would have made use of that information. I hope those thoughts would have been little seeds planted into my subconscious that would have grown and helped me see better ways to play this game called life at an much earlier age.

This is just one older human's views of how things might be better. If you agree with any of it, that's up to you. If it helps you, that's even better. If you don't agree with some of it, just consider that part comedy and I hope you get a good laugh out of it. Just remember that it might help you in the future when the need comes up or your life situation changes. Are there folks out there that are light years ahead of this, you can bet there are. Like I said at the beginning, this is for children and folks that don't yet have *Common Sense* "yet" and need it.

I have seen life from many points of view. Like most, a child, a youngest brother, a student, a husband, a father, a son, a friend, a lover, a worker and a boss and more!

I have picked up bottles as a kid (for money back when they were worth 3 cents apiece), cut grass, raked leaves, had a paper route, sorted eggs at a chicken farm, washed dishes at a Shoney's when they first opened (until 4 in the morning), been a busboy, a waiter, a bell boy, pumped gas (back when they did it for you), done construction (before they used nail guns), hand dug and hand built septic tanks, worked as a temporary employee in a metal foundry, been a machinist, a car mechanic, a bartender, a carpenter, a painter, a roofer, a block mason, done plumbing and electrical, have been an offshore fisherman, a shrimper, dug footings, poured concrete, hung drywall, built cabinets and fine furniture, built decks and docks, done rot and termite repair, been a logger, cleared land, worked with sawmills making lumber and owned my own small construction business and have been the main employee for more than 40 years. There's more, I just don't remember it all right now.

The point in bringing all of that up is that all of these jobs have helped me to see life and other people from many different perspectives as well as taught me many lessons. Another reason for mentioning these things is to show that there are many ways to make an income. Just try new things and don't be afraid to do something different, as long as you make sure to be safe while doing it. However if you get really good grades in school you may just get better work that doesn't wear the body out as much as manual labor. So decide as soon as possible whether you want to work with your body or your mind for a living.

My motto is; do things right the first time if you possibly can, safety first, quality second and quantity third. Because if you do things in that order, everyone gets to go home as healthy as they came to work. If you get the first two correct then the third will come naturally.

Like most, I didn't start out with these thoughts. I learned them from repeated mistakes. Life's way of teaching us what works and what doesn't. Remember what I said earlier about mistakes! The only person that isn't making any mistakes is the person that is not doing anything and he's making the mistake of not growing and living life to its fullest. We all make mistakes constantly. The trick is to fix them as soon as possible and learn from them.

Sometimes we hear things that we don't understand at the time, or that we don't want to understand at the time. After all; ignorance is bliss! Because, once we see the truth, not using it properly turns ignorance into stupidity. Now it is a choice and once we allow ourselves to continue to do things that we know are wrong, then we have to face the fact that we are making a conscious effort to keep making the same mistakes over and over. This holds back our future growth unnecessarily.

If we always do the same things and expect different results, we will just go in endless circles. We have been trying it our way, all of our life. If it is not working as good as you would like it to, wouldn't a new approach or an adjustment to that way be welcomed? This is the bulk of *Common Sense*, step back and really look at what you are doing that is not working to gain a better view of it.

I am constantly working on all of these things. I know that starting late in life to correct this is partially from a life of being socially conditioned before I saw thru the smoke and mirrors. Figuring most of this out on your own is quite time consuming. I hope these thoughts help others figure it out much sooner.

Have you ever built a snowman? You start with a snowball. You keep rolling it around on the ground letting it gather more snow it gets bigger and bigger. As long as you keep rolling it, it is fairly easy to keep moving. Then you stop for a minute to catch your breath or grab a drink of water, you come back and try to start the ball rolling again, only now it has a flat spot on it from sitting too long and it might be refrozen to the ground. If you left it small, it may not be too hard to get moving again. If you left it big enough to be the base of the snowman, you may find it a bit harder to get the ball rolling again and move it to where you want it. The moral here is to keep your life or projects moving forward until it is at a natural stopping point so it is easier to keep the whole project moving.

Life is a lot like that, as long as you keep the ball (the situations and projects in your life) rolling, it is always easier to keep them moving. If you walk away from them for too long, it might take a lot more effort just to get them moving again. The point is that you can almost always slow down to see how things are going, but it is wise to not ignore what you have started in the middle of it and leave it completely alone for too long. Keep the ball, (the projects in your life), moving forward even if it's slow and you won't spend a lot of wasted time just getting them moving again.

That being said, there are some things in life that need to rest awhile before continuing with them. Like the foundation of a building, you need to let the concrete set up good before you start to add weight to it. New relationships are like that, let them come together in your life naturally, without hurry and allow them to show themselves worthy of your time and effort. Once again, *Common Sense* will help you to determine these things.

This book is a lot like that. I experienced something similar to a writer's block during both the writing and the editing and had trouble moving forward. I do feel that this current version is way ahead of the original draft. I should have already been done with it, even though I am running a business, dealing with health issues, finishing my house, helped Mom with end of life issues and still trying to find time to spend with family and friends so that I can enjoy life as well.

I still could have made more time to finish this much earlier. Then came the hernia, two cataract surgeries, a direct hit from hurricane Matthew with a flood (8" of water in my downstairs) a fire (in the breaker panel), tons of tree removal, a kidney stone (that had to be surgically removed through the natural opening). Then another direct hit from hurricane Irma the next year, and more tree removal along with 6 stitches in the right hand and then another hernia on the other side all in 5 years. That will keep you on your toes or slow you down a bit like it did to me.

Yes, my own advice keeps haunting me but that is why you are even reading this now. Nobody said it was easy. The point is to never give up.

Let's talk about forward motion for a minute. Our bodies were designed to almost always stay in motion and our minds almost always thinking except for sleeping and meditating. We had to always follow the food source in the beginning of mankind because there was no grocery store. The food moved and we had to follow it. Our brains had to always be on the move and ready for anything good or bad. These traits are still in your DNA and you would be wise to not ignore them and sit too long doing nothing. Back then if you sat too long doing nothing and not paying attention, you might just become food for something else.

It is still the same today, in east India in 2014 a man was crabbing with his son and daughter and a Bengal Tiger jumped onto the boat and grabbed him by the neck, flung him over his back and jumped back into the woods and disappeared as fast as he came. In the urban jungle you can be robbed, attacked or murdered just as easy. In the corporate jungle you can be on top one day and left completely behind and bankrupt the next. In the jungle of love your best friend could fall in love with your significant other and lure them away overnight.

Always be aware of your surroundings, people included, and always stand ready to make adjustments at a moment's notice. Remember, it is almost always: survival of the fittest and the smartest. Be ready for changes to happen and roll with the punches of life without letting them knock you out. Look for happiness and let problems fall by the wayside instead of holding onto them longer then it takes to find a solution. Don't turn them into grudges and feuds. Laugh at the lesson if you can and move on, or even have a quick scream or a cry, but keep it as short as possible. Not knowing this as I grew up, I had a tendency to hold a grudge until I finally figured out that the only one it was hurting was me.

For some, these words may have no meaning. However, I hope they will at least give rise to thoughts of your own that will head you in a direction that will be beneficial to you.

A greater number of people with a conscious awareness of *Common Sense* and positive intentions towards the betterment of all mankind can surely help. That is the place in my mind that the thoughts in this book come from. I hope you enjoy reading it and contemplating making your own life better.

For what it is worth, I'm 68 and still a work in progress. All of these things confront me regularly but at least I have this information to help me make better decisions and find my way as I move through this lifetime.

Now I make more time for myself for yoga, meditation, deep thinking, walking, making better food choices and basically just taking better care of me. I am worth it and so are you, please make time for yourself starting now. Cut TV time out or at least in half, the same with phones, games and social media. Now you have all the "me" time that you need, enjoy it.

Become comfortable in your own skin. Learn to appreciate time you spend alone for these activities. Hang out with your favorite animal, listen to music that inspires you. We are able to be our self when we are alone. Be playful, be serious or be just whatever you feel like being without anyone around to judge you for your actions. You will find out more about yourself being alone than you ever will by being with others. So learn to appreciate your alone time. I love me, do you love you?

CHAPTER 5
COMMON SENSE
IN THE HOME

There are more things in our care than other humans. So the discussion of places and things is also necessary. *Common Sense* says we might want to keep our homes as clean as possible, repaired, warm or cool and inviting, just to create a more comfortable living environment.

There are very few people that want to walk into a complete mess of a home and say; gee it's good to be back here, I miss this place. However, I'm sure there are some. I like to imagine that most folks would like to live in a nice, clean and comfortable home, even if it's a cave.

Why clean and the least amount of clutter? *Common Sense* says that clean is less likely to hold germs, insects, rodents and other disease carrying varmints. You don't have to go overboard to be clean, of course, unless you want to and it makes you happy.

However, take the trash out when the can is full and before it starts to stink. You would be surprised to know how many people I've seen walk right by an overflowing trash can in their kitchen.

Keep the kitchen relatively clean to keep bugs down and germs away. Throw out those science projects growing in the refrigerator. Empty the toaster on occasion and clean the microwave oven, refrigerator, stove, sink and dishwasher. It really doesn't take that long to sweep and vacuum the floor and cleanup if you make it a daily or at least weekly habit. Or you can just hire a maid if you can afford it.

Why should we keep our homes orderly? This doesn't mean, a place for everything and everything in its place, unless you want it that way. Just not stuff stacked up knee-deep so you can't find the dog and cat.

In general, the more orderly our place is, or at least our own order, the easier it is to find things. We are less apt to lose things. And of course, it is usually much safer to move around when you're in a hurry with your hands full. It is also safer when the power goes out at night and you can't see where you are going.

Keeping the home and things in it in good repair is wise. If it's broken or doesn't work right, fix it or replace it or at least throw it away before it hurts someone. If it's something that has to wait to be fixed, at least put it away until it is fixed and if it still has to be used, do so with extreme caution. The hospitals and morgues are full of people that got hurt at home because of a faulty item. Using *Common Sense* might just keep you from being one of them.

Fix the loose step and pick up the toy or paper in the floor before someone falls because of it. Patch the leak in the roof, fill the hole in the yard, simple stuff, you get the idea. Taking small steps to take care of your home will help prevent major problems.

I have done home repairs professionally for over 40 years. You have no clue how many homes I have fixed because someone would not use *Common Sense* and take notice of a water leak and have it fixed before it caused the problem.

I know of a fast food restaurant where the toilet in the men's room ran for over three months and may still be running. The wasted water alone would have paid for the repair and yes I told them about it.

I have seen toilets that literally fell through the floor, washing machines as well. I have seen floors so bad that you had to walk on the floor joists, just to keep from falling through the floor. *Common Sense* says that if it has to be fixed, sooner is always better and cheaper than later.

The question in some cases isn't always, was this a lack of *Common Sense*? Sometimes people just get lazy and in some cases they either don't know any better or just don't care and sometimes just can't afford it yet. We get back to the point of: why isn't *Common Sense* taught in school, in the home and all the way through life?

All human beings should know the basics of life. Like how to wipe their own butts, feed and dress their self, keep clean and even "be responsible for their own actions."

But, I digress! We are still "in the home". Just to reiterate, a home that is comfortable and nice and inviting, even if we live alone and if for no other reason than to maintain personal happiness is almost always preferable! Most people are happier in a clean, nice, warm and inviting home. I said most, not all! However, it does seem to show a bit more personal respect for one's self. That is, unless you just happen to love living in a mess.

That is why we have freedom of choice.

CHAPTER 6
ALPHA
PERSONALITIES

In every relationship, business and household there is the alpha male or alpha female. We will just call them the alpha personality. They seem to put themselves in charge of everybody else because someone has to be the leader in most groups. I believe that puts them in charge of needing to use the most *Common Sense*. However, everybody should be responsible to use it as much as humanly possible regardless of your role in life.

As alpha personalities we like to think that "our" way is the best way. With some alpha personalities, it's the "only" way. We also seem to think that everybody concerned with our decisions should be completely happy to do their part with a smile or at least just do their part. It doesn't always work that way.

The older I get and the more I listen to wise self help teachers, the more I realize that others aren't always thrilled to see things the same way, especially other alpha personalities! In the end everybody's right way is different and most of them will work to some degree.

We all have to listen to someone and we aren't always glad to hear what they have to say and rarely do many of us agree on the same things. Now remember this, almost all bosses, law enforcement officers, politicians, parents and persons in charge, are alpha personalities. Multiple alpha personalities involved in the same plan often creates conflict. However they can all cooperate and work together if they try.

So, as the old saying goes: "why can't we all just get along"? Why all the drama, power plays and chest pounding arguments? Why can't we just agree to be able to disagree? Everybody's opinion does not have to be the same. There is usually an answer that will work for the majority. This lesson usually takes awhile to learn, at least it has for me and I am still working on it.

Here is where *Common Sense* should prevail. However, that's where greed, selfishness, closed mindedness, our ego, the desire to be the most powerful, and of course the one who thinks that they are right comes in and ruins everything. We have all done it. Have you ever screwed something up? The trick is to fix it as soon as possible.

Why are we all so afraid of being wrong? "The only people that don't make mistakes are the ones that aren't doing anything" and they are making the mistake of not growing. Being wrong is not a big problem as long as you are willing to stick around and make it right and haven't hurt anyone.

I was afraid of publishing this book and being judged by people that did not see *Common Sense* in a similar way that I do at this time, because even my thoughts on *Common Sense* changes sometimes daily. I may look back a year from now and wonder just what the heck was I thinking. So, I edited it with help from friends that read it and made good suggestions about the order of information and the content. Then I rewrote it for close to five years, just trying to get the content close enough for most people to relate to. *Common Sense* changes for all of us constantly as the world shows us better ways to use it.

The first thing you have to do is actually *want* more *Common Sense* in your life. Believe it or not there are some that don't or just don't care yet. Ignorance can be bliss if that is all you want out of your life. Life will be a lot more fun if you learn new things constantly.

In some cases there has to be a standard that works for the masses and that is quite understandable. What happens on a smaller scale does not have to be all that difficult. Sometimes it just comes down to what is right for the given situation. In the end even the alpha personalities should listen to the *Common Sense* of that. The bottom line is if you are wrong, it does not matter who you are, admit it, make it right and move on.

I have learned that when I make a plan that requires help and ask for it, only to find no one willing, then demanding someone else who I think owes me a favor or I think should help me my way isn't always realistic. This is another place where *Common Sense* needs to be present.

Most of the time it is best to make it worth someone's time to help you. You can offer to barter time or things but offering to pay usually works best. You can offer to teach along the way if it is something that interests your potential helper. All of these things and more can create cooperation. We all like to feel like we got something (other than stiffed) out of the deal.

Alpha personalities can use this to get the things that have to be done accomplished and still keep the bulk of the group feeling positive. However, there can always be a lazy individual who just doesn't care or doesn't see things the same way. You may have to improvise there. If you force people to do what you want, they may do it, but if they are unhappy about it they will rarely do their best. It may also come back to bite you in the butt.

So, how do we keep almost everybody on our team happy? Start by putting yourself in their shoes and ask yourself how you would feel having to do what you have asked them to do. If you wouldn't like to have to do it, then you may need to step up and help create a situation that works for most of the group, preferably everyone in the group.

Or, like I just mentioned, pay them or reward them in a way that makes it easier for them to agree with you. Anything short of that borders on mental or physical stress for that person, because they will most likely be miserable while doing what you have asked.

If we all put ourselves in the place of the person or people that we asked to do something, so that we feel what they might be feeling. There would probably be fewer negative results. Most people will do what is necessary as long as there is good reason and/or just rewards. Sometimes the reward is just being part of a happy group, family or team. In those cases we should always do our best as well. Having regular meetings with your family or team always helps for clear communication.

The scenario of leaders asking people to do what those same leaders don't want to do is basically what's wrong with the political arena around the world today. World leaders are asking people they represent to do things that those people do not want to do or feel like it is not right to do. Most of the time those leaders are asking people to do things that they would not do themselves.

Look at the results of leaders not using *Common Sense*. Look at all of the wars as well as all the peaceful and not peaceful demonstrations that are going on right now all around our world. It usually boils down to the fact that the alpha personalities in charge do not care how their decisions affect the very people whom they are leading. This is when they need to be replaced with leaders that care about the people they represent.

Alpha personalities look around you. Are the bulk of your subjects happy? Is almost everyone getting most of their needs met? If you are the only one happy in your group, you just might be wrong.

On a national scale this is not completely possible. You just can't please all the people all of the time. On a smaller scale it has more potential. If there are people on your team who are miserable, and you are the alpha personality, you are responsible for helping them to feel and live better at least about what you are asking them to do.

Notice that I did not say happier! We are all individually responsible for our own happiness. Happiness comes naturally when we feel good about ourselves and have a decent life. True happiness comes from inside of us and it is a choice that we make daily to be happy. Yes you can just wake up each day and choose to be happy. Things might change as the day goes by but you can always start it off being happy.

Sometimes the alpha personality in charge is incapable of caring how his decisions affect others. That is when people have to stand up and take charge for themselves. That's what started the American Revolution and the United States of America itself, *Common Sense* that there has to be a better way.

World consciousness is expanding at a rate never seen before. The internet and social media are helping to lead the way. More and more people are realizing that the negative aspects of greed, hate, cruelty and power mongering are just plain wrong for the whole of mankind.

The house of cards, of the non-caring alpha personalities in charge, is falling apart at a rate faster than ever before. They are losing their control over the masses as we wake up and see reality. So, alpha personalities, before your group mutinies on you and you find yourself hiding in a cave like Saddam Hussein, it may just be time to use some *Common Sense* and ask yourself: "Am I being fair and reasonable to most of the people most of the time? Would I like to be on the other end of my own rulings?" These questions should be asked all the way down to the relationship between a child and his pet. Any kind of abuse is wrong.

Saddam might still be president of Iraq had he changed his ways a long time ago. You have to ask yourself; what price am I willing to pay to keep total control in an evil manner? This goes for spouses, lovers, teachers, clergy, politicians, military, police, teachers, parents and even friends.

People that are in charge that treat other humans fairly and with respect are loved and their followers will do almost anything they ask. They will almost always reelect them as well.

Let's ask the question: "how can we be better supervisors, leaders, parents, politicians, teachers and persons in charge to as many people around us as possible?

How do we end the suffering of the masses? How can we apply and use more *Common Sense*?" Because some of you that are reading this book will one day become those leaders and the people that follow you will depend on it.

In reality there is enough positive energy, money, and happiness to go around. We only need a fairer way to distribute it and more people to wake up to the possibility of it. I don't mean just give it to people that don't earn it in one way or another or that just want it for free. Everyone should get their fair share for the effort that they put out. Actually, if we study and work consistently, maintain good health, strive to do better, meditate and focus on being happy, we will attract the positive energy and the people that we need around us to create the life that we want.

Let there be *Common Sense*, Love and fairness for all!

CHAPTER 7
COMMON SENSE
AT WORK

So, you have a job, congratulations! A lot of people don't. Do you like it? Some do, some don't. However, if you are getting paid to do it, then you owe your employer a fair hour of work for an hour of pay. You also owe it to your fellow employee's, or they are carrying your dead weight. You owe it to the company itself, so it can turn a profit and be able to afford to pay you. You owe it to the customer, so they will come back and do business yet again. Last, but not least, you owe it to yourself, so that you will have feelings of self-worth. Besides, no one likes a lazy worker. On the opposite end of that, do not let yourself be overworked, taken advantage of or abused at work.

Now, while you're at work, you need to completely put forth the effort to carry your share of the weight of the job. That starts with leaving any personal problems at home, where they belong. Work is not the place for them. Don't come in if you are sick, unless it's crucial that you be there! Then try to keep from getting anybody else sick. Don't shake hands, hug, touch others or let anybody eat or drink from your plate or cup. It's not fair to get anyone else sick too. Wear a mask if you are coughing or sneezing a lot and you work with other people.

While we're on the subject of work, a thought comes to mind, one of the first boss men that I had once told me: "If you don't want your feelings hurt, leave them at home. If you bring them to work, someone is going to step on them". Drama and attitudes should stay at home as well.

Remember this; there is usually one person that likes to stir crap up just to see if they can get under your skin. Do not fall for it, act as if you don't care and they will usually go away looking for someone else to mess with. They get off getting under someone else's skin and getting them riled up but if they get no response, they move on. Better yet management needs to deal with them or fire them as it is basically verbal bullying.

One thing to remember when dealing with an upset customer! Sometimes they are just upset with the company, and you are the company representative. So don't take it too personal. That is, unless it was you that caused the problem. Then just apologize and try and make it right as soon as possible.

One of the all-time biggest issues at work is, *SAFETY*. Safety is crucial for everyone's sake. Yours, your fellow employees, the public, the job itself and the company! Because if one person gets hurt, that day's efforts and progress are set back needlessly! If you do something wrong, fix it as soon as possible, or tell someone in charge immediately. It might be your own neck or job that you save.

Safety issues can be as simple as leaving out an important part. Something that is left on the floor that can be tripped over and causes a fall. A piece of equipment that isn't working properly or a fellow employee doing things in a way that is not right or safe. The hospital and graveyards are full of people that thought they could cheat a little, cut a corner, or just tried something stupid.

I have been the boss and safety officer on my jobs for over 40 years and we have not had a serious accident and I intend to keep it that way. I have always put myself in the most dangerous situations instead of a worker so that if something happens, it's me that takes to brunt of it and yes, I have had a few stitches but at least my workers didn't get hurt.

My motto is: "**safety first**, quality second and quantity third." Because if someone gets hurt, quality and quantity don't mean anything! And if you get the first two things right, quantity will come naturally. Everyone is supposed to get to go home in the same health that they came to work in. STAY alert and STAY alive.

We seem to blunder through life until we have those, light bulb over the head moments and we say; "oh wow, that's the way it's supposed to work." This is the quandary of the human experience. It doesn't have to be this way. We can help those around us to see these things earlier if we just talk more about the *Common Sense* ways of life.

Another reason to do your best at work is to learn more and make yourself more valuable to the company, which will help you to be in a place for a raise or promotion or both. The more you know and learn about your job and the company, the more valuable you will you become to the company and to yourself. Never stop learning.

Don't just learn about your own job. Try to learn as much as you can about other positions in the company, and the company's products as well.

Treat every day at work as an opportunity for advancement. Learn about the company's customers, so that you can help find ways for your company to cater to them. This is what keeps them coming back and buying more.

Try to learn something new every day. It will make the day go by faster. It will put you in a better mood and help you to feel good about yourself. This alone will carry over into the rest of your life and help you move forward even faster or to find a better job.

If another worker is down and not getting much done, throw them a kind word or a helping hand. If the boss has a problem and you have a potential answer to it, volunteer it, the worst they can do is say no for whatever reason and thanks for the effort. At least you are trying. Who knows, one time you just might have the right answer.

Keep your own work area clean, organized and properly stocked so that you will be efficient. Safe, efficient and productive are what companies look for. It is what makes you stand out, and bosses take notice of that.

They also take notice that you are on time and don't call in sick too often. They take notice of the opposite of these things as well. However, you will not like the results. You are either an asset to the company or you are not. They know which one you are. If you are being lazy and do poor work, they know it. As a matter of fact, they are probably looking for your replacement right now.

Never let yourself think that you are not replaceable. The company got along without you before you got there and it will probably get along just fine if you leave. When you get to work, actually be there. Turn your phone off and only answer calls on your break time, not the company's time unless your position actually gives you that luxury! But even then, don't abuse that privilege. Be a team player. Try your best to get all of your work done for that day. Focus on the job at hand and do it right.

Make a difference and keep a positive attitude. When you think that your job sucks, watch "Dirty Jobs," Mike Lowe has a way of showing you how to be grateful that your job isn't worse.

Look for ways to improve. Challenge yourself to constantly get better at what you do. You'll be a much better person all around because of your efforts.

Now, if you are doing "all" of these things. Feel free to go to the boss, in private, and ask for a raise. Never ask for a raise in front of other workers. It puts the boss on the spot and reduces your chances of getting it. If more money isn't something that your boss can offer, ask what perks and benefits may be available. Both are as good as money.

Always participate in the company's retirement program and match the funds the company allows. You will be glad you did when you retire.

If you are being the best "you", that you can be, and the best employee that you can be, you will always keep moving ahead in both your career and in your life.

That being said, always be looking for a way to start your own business if you think you are capable of it. Self-employment is a good feeling.

CHAPTER 8
AT SCHOOL

Common Sense at school is one basic concept. You are there to learn and if you are studying properly you won't have time to get in trouble. Socialize *outside* of the classroom. Give the teacher and the subject matter your full attention. And NO, I wasn't the perfect student. I should have tried harder. I wish someone would have explained to me *why* learning good study habits would be so beneficial later in life. I know it would have helped me get ahead much faster. I held myself back needlessly. Do you want to hold yourself back needlessly?

A good education in these fast-moving times is essential for most people. However there will always be those who are so inner driven, that they do not need much schooling. The rest of us need all the help and guidance we can get, both from the teacher and subject matter as well as from within. Within, means your inner voice. And it has two sides, negative and positive. The negative is your ego and the positive is your heart. We must learn to question the ego and follow the heart and find a balance that is fair to all concerned.

I personally wish I had tried harder while I was in school. I made excuses for not doing so and I may well have shortchanged myself in the process. I graduated high school in 1971 as the Viet Nam war was winding down. However most of the guys that weren't going to college were being drafted and many of them were coming home in caskets or wounded. I figured if that was going to be what happened to me then what was the point of going to school and making good grades and I spent more time enjoying life and hanging out with friends and dating. I actually ran off to the beach with a few friends that felt the same way and basically dropped out of school. BIG mistake folks believe me.

Then they came up with the ping pong ball lottery draft system and I was lucky enough to get a high enough number to not be drafted. So now I had to get myself back in school and make up for lost time because they cut my grades in half for being gone so long. Now I had to play catch up because most of the school year was over. I ended up graduating on time with decent grades but I could have stayed in school and just enjoyed my evenings and weekends more and done better for myself. Always look at your situation from all sides and ask for help before making a big mistake like I did.

We should not make excuses that allow us to let ourselves down. I have spent a lifetime working my body for a living when I could've been using my mind to make an even better living. Don't get me wrong I have enjoyed seeing what I can create with my mind and my hands. I even built my own house out of the materials from an old train station that we disassembled and brought back 100 miles and used that material to build it with. I have no idea just how much weight in materials I have lifted and carried in my life but I am 68 and still climb trees and work out.

An old friend reminded me once that you can make more money with a sharp pencil and sharp mind, than you can with a shovel and a strong back.

Try to be an asset to your school and fellow students. Reach out and help others when you can, or at least study and don't distract other students or teachers.

Encourage others to do their best and not act out or bully fellow students. If you are having problems at school, at home or just with your thoughts. Talk to a counselor, teacher or friend you can trust that you know is fair and honorable. Always start with small things until you know this person has your back in all ways. Never divulge your deepest secrets unless you are completely sure of someone and then still be careful and ask yourself if you need to speak about it. There are some things we just need to keep to our self.

If you need additional help learning, speak up, ask for help. Don't waste time not learning because you feel too embarrassed to ask for help. Use any of the many computer search engines to assist yourself with definitions or how things work. They are an infinite source of information. Just remember, even they can be wrong on certain issues. So cross check everything.

Don't worry about getting into specific social cliques, focus on your studies and you will find your own group along the way. You will know when you have found good friends because it will just feel right in your heart when you are with them. If it doesn't feel right, just keep moving. I'd rather be alone than spending time with people with negative attitudes or that I don't get along with just to have company.

Good grades equal more money and a better job and more opportunities for your future. It also means a more intelligent *you*.

I have very few true friendships that lasted from school. Most of my real friends I found as I journeyed on through life. So, just keep moving forward. True friends will come at the right time.

Don't get me wrong. Make time for your true friends, just not when you need to be learning. Because a good social network is essential as well! Do your best to make real friends. Not just the cool people, athletic stars, or the best looking. That is, of course, unless these people happen to be your good friends. Remember that it is better to have a few really good friends more so than a large group of people you barely know that might not really care about you.

If something makes you feel bad or you have negative feelings while you are doing it, then it might be wrong for you at this time. It's okay to try something new and different. However, you should feel good about it while you're doing it. Unless you are hurting someone and then no matter what you are doing it is wrong unless you are backed into a corner and have no other way out.

Watch what people do more so than what they say. Their actions tell you the truth no matter what comes out of their mouth. Let's say your friend says or does something that makes you feel bad then it probably is bad, at least for you! However, call them on it, ask them: "why did you do or say that?" It should make them think about it and just may encourage better behavior in the future. If they won't change it may be time to make new friends.

Here is something that deserves its own paragraph. "Human beings *always make time* for what they truly want to do. So if they say that they want to spend more time with you and they don't, then they didn't really mean it. Just go make better friends or keep working on a better you.

Ask your true friends to call you on your questionable behavior. It will teach you to think things through, before you act or speak unwisely. Ask yourself daily if you feel that you are doing your best. If not, look inside yourself to see what you need to do. The answer is always there, it just may take some thinking to see it.

If you want to try something new and it feels right, and hurts no one, or the planet and its inhabitants, then try it. Like they say; fake it till you make it, and that has worked for many people. If it still feels right, just monitor it to make sure it stays that way because even the best of our intentions can go wrong.

Choose and practice subjects and activities that challenge you and make you think and push your limits. Also, keep doing easy ones to keep your confidence up. Make time each day for exercise, meditation and deep breathing practices as well and do them daily or as often as you can. These things are good for the body, the mind and the brain. Do not neglect your spirit as it needs loving care as well!

If you do not yet know what you want to do with your life at the moment, and don't feel comfortable asking for help, then read about the things that interest you and watch videos of those things. Then try to imagine yourself doing those things and see how that feels to you. Participate in new activities to see how you feel about them. What you enjoy and what works for you is constantly changing so do your best to be flexible.

Also, read men's or women's health type magazines and articles to expand your knowledge of the mind, body and finances. Learn how to take care of your mind, body and your money. You only get one body and one chance to get your body through this life. The better you take care of it, the happier you will be and the more energy you will have and the more confident you will become. Do your best with what you have and always look for ways to improve.

We are here to enjoy the human experience. If you find that you are not enjoying yours, STOP, find something to feel good about and that makes you happy. Listen to your favorite music, watch a good movie, hang out with a friend you enjoy being with. Plant a flower, pet your favorite pet, take a road trip, go for a walk, ride a bike or anything that makes you feel good that doesn't hurt anyone.

Just surround yourself with things that make you happy as much as you can. Move towards them and away from things that don't make you happy. Just try to find something to be happy about daily. Intend love, health, happiness, prosperity, safety, peace of mind and speak of your intentions daily. Speak your appreciation for these things every day even if they are not completely here for you yet.

Always remember to thank those that help to make your life better and give back to them as you can.

Just remember the golden rule: "Do onto others as you would have them do unto you."

You also have the responsibility to look around you to see if what you are doing to make yourself happy is hurting anybody else.

I have always wondered why we humans don't ask ourselves: "When does my happiness get to be someone else's misery?" It should not. Try to make sure that it doesn't.

Try your best to keep a positive attitude. If you find yourself feeling bad around certain people or situations, find new people to be around and new things to do.

Look for new ways to love yourself and new ways to improve your life. If you stay positive and keep at it, the doors will open. The teachers will come.

School should be a good, enjoyable, learning experience. If yours isn't, ask for help!

A last thought on school from a *Common Sense* perspective, parents should ask their children what they are interested in and help them to learn these things to see if they are really interested in them. If they are interested then practice will make them good at it. Parents should not blindly shove their kids into something that the parent wants the child to do, especially if the child is miserable trying it.

We should create learning centers that help all children to find their hidden talents and passions. It would be a place that teaches all areas of life, music, science, sports, art, nature and teachings of all kinds.

The child comes in with parents, take a visual and verbal aptitude quiz to see what areas of interest that they already have. Then go into these areas just looking at them all and see what they are naturally drawn to. Then encourage them to participate in these activities, with and without the parents to see if their parents have influence over the child's choices. Allow them to move freely between activities to also encourage natural curiosity in as many subjects as possible.

The worst thing a parent can do is make their child do what they did growing up especially if the child does not like it. Yes it is natural for a parent to share what they liked but as soon as you see that your child has no interest then you should back off and help them to find what they really like to do what makes them happy. Always ask the child just what interests them the most and remember even that will change as they grow up.

So let's recap this chapter. I know that most folks will not use ½ of what is taught in school after graduating and in real life. I feel the best part for most people will be; learning how to socialize properly and how to make new friends (just make sure they are serious about being your friend and always have your back and support your path), otherwise just move on. It helps with learning to read and write better and with retaining more useful information. Math is essential (just so you can count your money LOL). You learn how to make a routine work for you. They offer sports if you have athletic abilities and some schools offer music, art and shop if you are interested. These things can broaden your awareness of life and lead you into fun situations.

If you pay close attention you will learn a lot about Human Relations just by watching what people do compared to what they say. That alone is priceless to know. School can be very useful if you use it in these manners.

Do your best to make good grades in all classes because it will increase your brain power in all areas. Make good use of your time in school while growing up and then being an adult will be easier for you. You will know that you are doing it right when you enjoy and look forward to going to school.

MICHAEL GOODYEAR

Notes to Self

CHAPTER 9
DRIVING

I am not a perfect driver but I do follow some pretty basic *Common Sense* rules of the road that a lot of drivers seem to be oblivious of.

Seatbelts nowadays are a no-brainer. It's the law anyway. So just do it.

Turn signals, they are there for a reason. Use them! How is anybody going to know what you're about to do if you don't use them? I see so many people that don't even use them at all. Unless you are in a turn only lane, you should use them. You should use them to change lanes as well. Besides, in some states, it's a four-point violation if they pull you over for it, ask me how I know that lol.

Please try not to impede the flow of traffic. If you want to drive slower than the speed limit at least pull over and let the other cars go by. If you're on a four lane, move to the slow lane as soon as you can.

There are so many drivers who drive like they are the only people on the road. If you want to drive 35 mph in a 55 mph zone, at least look behind you and make sure that you're not holding up a half a mile of traffic.

On the interstate, if you want to drive slower, then please stay in the right-hand lane unless you are passing or are the only car on the road. When you pass another slow car, speed up a little and get around them quickly. Don't drive beside them for a mile trying to pass them only 1 MPH faster than they are moving so you don't hold up traffic.

You are an accident just waiting to happen if you are in the passing lane and only going the speed limit or less. And I don't have a clue where all of the "Slower Traffic Keep Right" signs have gone. Please bring them back.

Please don't tailgate. Especially when you can see that,

A. The driver in front of you is already behind another car that they can't pass.

B. When they are doing the speed limit and you can see they don't want to go any faster. They usually like their drivers license and want to keep it. Pass them safely, when you can.

Try to be a courteous driver and help the other drivers trying to get into traffic. On a four lane, if you see someone trying to pull out, and you are in the right-hand lane, and you can get into the left-hand lane safely, do so and let them get on the road as well. Basically, do the same thing for anyone else that you would appreciate if they did for you.

Road rage! Will you really remember the driver that cut you off or pulled out in front of you a week from now? Probably not! Why not just chalk it up to the fact that you have probably done it to someone else. Or that you might one day do-it-yourself and just let it go right then. Let's keep the highways safe for all of us. Learn all the rules of the road and use them.

I'll keep this one short. Because, it's hard to listen to anyone tell us how to drive. Just be careful, safe and respect the other guy as much as you want to be respected yourself. Share the road, we all have to use it and road rage just isn't worth your time.

CHAPTER 10
FINANCES

I had a paper route as a kid. I did odd jobs, cut grass and even picked up bottles when they had a 3 cent return on them. I knew how to make money but I didn't know how and why to save some of it. I had pockets full of real silver dimes, quarters, half dollars and even occasional silver dollars. Even a lot of wheat pennies! If I had saved 10% of that, it would be sweet to have today, not to mention what all that silver would be worth.

What better time to learn how to budget, save and deal with something we will be handling and dealing with all of our lives, than when we are young.

Because, when we are really young, we don't really need or want to buy much. What better time to develop a healthy attitude towards saving money. At a young enough age, we can fascinate children with the possibilities of having their money "work" for them. If we just get that through to them, that alone might inspire them to develop a lifelong habit of paying themselves first. Teach your child to put at least 10% aside and not touch it except for emergencies. Always try to keep a rainy day fund.

Being in construction, and hiring laborers, you have no idea how many guys that I have paid on Friday only to find them asking for an advance on next week's pay on Monday, just for lunch and gas. Very few people understand the need to create a budget and make themselves live within it. If you have no knowledge of how or why you need to save your money, so that it can work for you, it will always keep slipping through your fingers. If you always find yourself broke then write down what you spend so you can see where your money is going, all the way down to buying a snack. It's the only way to track your spending habits. That way you can see where you can make changes.

Children are like little sponges, begging to absorb knowledge and discipline but only if we catch them early enough. It must be before they learn of all the new shiny play toys that money will buy for them or all the sweet candy and sodas that they can get with it!

Teach children early that toys often break and candy and sodas might taste good but they are not good for you and they can completely destroy your health when they are eaten too often or if they are eaten at all in some cases.

Keep children's earliest play toys in a box, so you can show them that they not only outgrow them and lose interest in them, but show them that they also break and become useless very easy. Then the money that was spent on them goes to the dump. Never to be seen again.

You can also help them to recycle them on eBay or Craigslist. That will show them ways get some of the money back for newer things that they like to do now and how quickly that they have outgrown the old ones. Try to get children interested in educational toys and games so that they learn from playing. At least donate the old toys and games instead of throwing them in the dump when the child loses interest in them.

Teach them early, the truth that we now know about sugar so they don't spend a lot of money all through their lives on it and the products that it is in. Teach children that too much sugar is actually poisonous for the body. It's one of the leading causes of obesity. It's bad for your teeth. It's hard on your digestive system. Too much of it can lead to diabetes. Teach them that sodas are loaded with sugar and high fructose corn syrup, artificial flavors, food coloring and that those things are bad for their health.

Show children just how much sugar is in the snacks that they ask for and show them healthy alternatives like fruit, vegetables, seeds and nuts. Also make sure they understand that they can have an allergy or sensitivity to some foods and that they should stay away from those foods. I explain more about that later in the book.

The money they save on these things alone will be a staggering amount over the years. If you buy a couple of sodas and some snacks everyday at a convenience store, that can get close to 5.00+/day x 365 days/year = $1825.00/year. And for older folks imagine if you add cigarettes on top of that at $5.00+/pack.

Show them older children and adults that have poor saving habits and why those people are always broke. Teach children to spend wisely, so that they spend their hard-earned money for things that last longer and make a difference in their lives.

Give children chores and jobs around the house at an early age and pay them for their efforts if you can. Make them earn their allowance. This will help teach them that money is worth saving and has value. It will also help to build their feelings of self worth.

As they grow up, help to guide them with the things that they buy. Set a rule that large purchases on toy type items, need a one week think it over period. During that time, ask them what else they might consider doing with that money. It will help them to learn not to impulse buy. Impulse buying is our worst enemy with our money. They might find out, on their own, that they don't want or need it as much as they thought they did.

So much for the kids! Let's talk about adults because kids grow up to be adults and need to know this. All of these same rules and guidelines apply to adults as well. It's just that now they need to be applied on a much broader scale. We not only need to think about our toys, but our daily living expenses and personal needs as well.

Information is everywhere now, all the time, so look for it when you need it. It is not a good thing when we get stuck with a bad product. Search product reviews of all the things you're going to buy, or most things to see if they hold up to the test of time. Ask department managers which brands never get returned and which ones do. That alone speaks volumes for a product.

Reviews of movies, restaurants, motels, electronics and stores are all over the Internet. Use them to help guide you. Be a know-ledgeable shopper. Take a minute to find the better product, the better store, the sale or at least the best price, unless, you're just in a hurry and rich or don't care. All of this determines how far your paycheck will go.

Use your money wisely. As the old saying goes; "a penny saved, is a penny earned." Also, don't drive across town to save a few cents per gallon on gas at another station. You will have lost your savings on the gas you buy, using the gas you already had to get there. Gas, time and wear and tear on the vehicle and tires are expenses as well. Factor that in as you go.

Don't make impulse runs to the store for one item. Keep a list most of the time. Plan trips to the different places you need to go, so they will be more productive. The price of gas and wear and tear on our cars can eat up a big piece of our paycheck as well. In this economy, we can't afford to be foolish with our time or our money. It is most times best to create a happy medium between what you want and what you need.

If something is about to break on your car or a tire is close to going flat or the battery is getting weak. Fix it, before, it breaks or leaves you on the side of the road in the rush hour traffic or causes an accident. Then you won't have to pay for a tow truck and be late for work or that important appointment or date. You will still have to spend that same money to fix it anyway after it breaks plus the inconvenience of the break down. The more efficient that you are with your money, the more of it you will keep. Foolish expenses add up fast.

Don't even try to keep up with your friends that have and make more money than you. They are spending their mad money. So stop when you're mad money runs out.

There is no shame in saying: I can't afford to do that. If your friends really want you along, they will chip in and help you out. You are better off going home while you still have money left in your pocket, unless it is something that you just have to do. Some experiences can be priceless.

When you are just starting out and don't have much money don't keep all of your money "on" you. This is where having a bank account really helps. Only take the money with you that you can afford to spend on what you are going to do unless you have great will power. Having your money in the bank will give you time, while you are going to the ATM or writing a check, to think about whether you really need to spend more money.

It is usually a good idea to stash an emergency $20 or $50 bill in a place in your wallet that you have to dig for it to get at it. That little bit of time is still enough to make you think. Should I spend this money? Is this really that important to me? That way, it will be there when you really need it for a true emergency or for that once in a lifetime chance to do that thing you always wanted to do if it fits your budget.

Try your best to live debt-free. If you have credit cards only put on your credit cards what you know you can pay off at the end of the month. If you have to use them for more than you can pay off at the end of the month, at least pay *way* more than the minimum due.

Credit cards are a great tool, if used properly. Use them wisely and they can help you. Use them wrong and they will break you.

Put most purchases that you will pay off at the end of that month on them because cash back reward points and Sky Miles add up at a faster rate than you think. Don't let money that you can get back slip through your fingers. Just be sure to pay off the balance at the end of the month. The interest you will pay will eat up your cash back quickly.

Stay in touch with your money. Go over all of your account balances, bills and statements, at least once a month. The pros say weekly or daily is better. Your money is more important to you than video games, TV, dating, movies and anything else that you can do without. Try not to spend yourself broke. If you know how you stand financially, you will make better decisions with your expenses.

Once I got married and had a family, I always told myself; the bills have to be paid first, there has to be gas in the cars and food in the kitchen and the family has to have what they need before I can spend money on anything else.

You also need a rainy day fund. The experts say one month expenses minimum, six months is better. However, if you're working paycheck to paycheck, this is something you will need to save for. Emergencies out of nowhere happen all too frequently. Looking back and wishing that you had not partied or played quite as much, so that you can cover what now needs cash to fix, just won't do it. Play in moderation until you have yourself covered financially! You can enjoy life without spending all of your money.

The earlier we get our expenses in control and our finances stabilized, the easier we can live. Be smart with your money and know your budget. **Financial harmony equals Financial Freedom!**

CHAPTER 11
HEALTH AND
EATING HABITS

When it comes to your health it is you that is in charge and makes the choices that affect it. Do not rely solely on doctors as they are taught disease management, not so much health care. They are good to fix a broken bone, stitch up a wound, operate if it is necessary and treat situations that have gotten completely out of control such as major diseases and many other things. They have their place but you will rarely hear one ask you about your lifestyle, eating habits, exercise routine or how much sleep you get. I have yet to hear one ask if I deep breath or meditate and try to keep stress out of my life. Some doctors will go that far but mostly they just ask you what is wrong and prescribe a medication. If they tell you that you have to take those medications for life then you really need to look at changing what you eat and drink as well as your lifestyle. JMHO

A lot of times you can control things like high blood pressure, high cholesterol, heartburn and indigestion, obesity and insulin resistance simply by changing what you eat, drink or ingest and increasing your level of activity. We need to take responsibility for our own health care so we will not need the medications. The choice is yours but a lot of people seem to choose the medications so they can keep the unhealthy lifestyle so choose wisely. You will see the results of your choice in the mirror in the near future whether it is a good choice or not.

Once again, you only get one life and one body to get through this life with. Good health, fitness and being happy can make it a lot easier to enjoy this life.

Be aware of things that abuse the body. Even though it seems like the body can come back from being abused and I say *seems* because if we abuse our body we leave a permanent scar *inside* it. The fact that it can heal is a good thing for all of us but just like being cut leaves a scar so does any damage we do to our inner body. Yes, I have many scars as well and I am sharing this in hopes it can help someone else grow older with many less scars.

Do your body a favor and try not to abuse it to start with and at least cut as far back as possible or even stop if you have been abusing your body.

If human beings would learn (at a very early age) to resist addictive substances, behaviors and thoughts, and instead study the practice of good health, happiness, inner peace, mindfulness, personal growth and achievement, their lives would improve at a rate that would astound them.

If we just give the body all the love, the good foods, the proper breathing and all the clean water that it needs and the exercise it wants to stay healthy, it will usually give you many years of good service.

Even if you let it go for a little too long and then give it those things with your best effort, it will usually respond wonderfully. Your body is a lot like a car. If you do your maintenance, change the oil, keep good tires on it, keep it clean and plenty of gas in it etc., well then it usually works really well and lasts longer. Your body needs the same attention.

Let's start with health and good eating habits. I wish someone would have told me this when I was a child. This is one subject that I know is not being taught very well to the masses from childhood and definitely not being taught in schools.

It is the practice of choosing the right foods for "your" body and your situation! We are all different and many things mean the difference between whether the food one person tolerates well may not work for another person without them having problems from eating the same foods.

So, let's consider the most basic aspects of health. You can live for weeks without food, days without water but only minutes without oxygen. This chapter will look at these things more completely but let's start with the basics.

Oxygen is the first basic need of life. It gives all the cells and organs of the body the most important component of life. Without oxygen, the cells will die in minutes. So, even if you sit most of the day, remember to breathe full deep breaths as often as you can and yes, sitting up straight like mom told you to is best LOL.

Water is the second most important need of our body. The body is mostly water and to let it become dehydrated is not good for it. So find out how much water you need for your body size and the situation you live in. Usually about ½ your body weight in ounces of water (150 lbs. = 75 ounces of water per day). Preferably filtered water to get most of the contaminants out of it and *never* drink from a hose. A hose sits outside in the sun most times and the water is stagnant in it for days at a time. Even if you flush it out, the inside walls of the hose are filthy. If it's the only source available at least unscrew the hose from the spigot and drink from straight from the spigot.

Being active hot and sweating usually demands more water than being cool and resting but always stay hydrated accordingly and always try to drink the right amount of water for your body weight per day or close to it.

You would be surprised how many people and workers I have seen go hours without drinking any water. Sometimes even I get too busy and forget to drink more water. Just do your best to remember to stay hydrated.

Good quality food is the third most important thing that your body needs. So choose your foods wisely and don't let your taste buds fool you into eating foods with no nutritional value. If your body does not look as healthy as it should, it is trying to tell you that you are not giving it everything that it really needs or that you might have a health issue. It could also be telling you that you are not getting enough water and exercise or that you might be sick.

If you only had these three things, your body could at least survive, just not as well as adding other important things that the mind, body and spirit needs.

Exercise is crucial for good health. Our bones and muscles were designed for it. Full body exercise like when you were a kid. Running, jumping, climbing, walking and staying active are all important. If you can't do some of these things, at least do as much as you can and imagine yourself improving constantly. Always see yourself getting better every day. Find ways to fit an extra stretch or squat into your day. It only takes a few seconds and it adds up over time. You may even find out that you prefer exercise and more knowledge instead of the distraction of social media and the TV.

Enjoying your life is also very important. If you are not enjoying yours then you should look very closely at what you are doing with your life. You can usually see why you are not enjoying it if you slow down and really step back and look at it objectively. Do not be in a hurry to get the true view of your life from all angles because as the saying goes; "appearances can be deceiving!" Always keep looking deeper and don't stop with the first thing that you find as it is probably only the beginning. Keep looking deeper and you will see even more about yourself that can help you.

Even if you cannot completely change what you are doing in your life, you can at least change the way you look at it. You can also change the way that you deal with it. It has to start somewhere and this can be the first step for you.

If it is something that others are doing to you that is keeping you from enjoying life then you can always ask someone that cares about you for help. Never let anyone bully or abuse you if you can find a way out of it. Speak up for yourself in a manner that won't piss off an abusive person. Tell them that they are causing you emotional or physical stress. Even if you just say; please stop. If they won't stop then you must look for a way out of that relationship. We all have options and we need to keep looking for better situations in our life to place our self.

We need to try to reduce any stress that we might have in our lives and make a better connection with universal energy. Even if we can't change what is happening to us, we can always just make up our minds to deal with it in a manner that lessens the effect of it on us. Remember to focus on the solution not the problem.

You can almost always react to things in many different ways. If, someone else is creating your stress, try asking them to stop and tell them why. Once again, if they won't stop, ask someone that does care about you for help or find new friends.

If you haven't started meditating yet it is a wonderful habit to start and keep for life. If you never have meditated you might start with one of the many guided meditations that you can find on YouTube. You can also just find a quiet place where you can be alone with your thoughts and sit and deep breathe. Focus on your breath and try to quiet your mind as to let new ideas come to you from the Universe.

So, let's recap this in a short version. Breathe deeply and exhale completely and often, drink plenty of good clean water *before* you get thirsty. Thirst is your body's last way of telling you that you are becoming dehydrated. Eat mostly good natural foods that benefit the body. Stay active everyday that you can. Be as happy as you can be and try to keep as much stress out of your life that you can. Meditate for at least 15 minutes a day. It doesn't take a lot of extra time and you are worth it. Just swap out some of your TV or goof off time to make a better connection with your body and your mind. I love you all and I know that we can all do these things. Daily practice of all of this will show you improvement on a regular basis so keep at it.

Let's look a lot deeper at the foods that we eat. Learn how *your* body uses food for fuel and you will make better food choices. If you want improvement then you will need all the good clean energy that you can get to stay motivated.

Learn what foods provide you with useful fuel for energy and what foods have only empty calories that drain you just to digest them. Learn what foods help *your* body and what foods hurt *your* body. Learn *your* food intolerances, food sensitivities and allergies. We all have them. They are different for everybody so research and find what works best for you.

Some people can die from eating a peanut, others from shell fish. Some people may just get rashes or indigestion, heartburn or diarrhea. The way you feel after eating something will usually warn you if there is a problem with that food for you. Pay attention to how *your* body uses different foods. Your body may use some food to make fuel for energy and other foods it may store as fat or both. We need our body to do both but at the right time and in the right order. It's *your* responsibility to find out what works for *your* body and what doesn't. It's *your* body and that makes it *your* responsibility if you want to improve.

After your shower stand in front of the mirror and take a good long look at yourself, then be honest with yourself and look for areas that you want to improve. Then ask yourself if you are ready to accept the challenge of maintaining a truly healthy body and a sharp mind. What you see in the mirror that you want to change can usually be done by changing your habits. As discussed above we can turn bad habits into good ones just by changing our minds.

We are experiencing an obesity epidemic that seems to be spiraling out of control. God help us if we don't get a grip on it. If you don't appreciate my reference to God, then you don't have to read this paragraph of the book. I am not a church going devout Christian. However, I am a spiritual, God loving human being. You may believe in a different higher power or none at all. That is your choice and it does not offend me. This is my choice, I hope it does not offend you and it shouldn't. I am not asking you to believe the same way that I do. Just allow me to have my beliefs. Again, these are only my own opinions of *Common Sense*. If you have better ideas, write a book too. I'll be glad to read it. I'll get off my soapbox now.

Remember our bodies were designed before grocery stores came along. Before bagged, boxed, packaged, canned, bottled, processed and manmade foods came into existence. If you will feed your body the things it was naturally designed to use, it will get closer to its normal condition a lot faster. You have to help with portion control, hydration (drinking enough water), exercise and sleep. Getting enough good sleep is also essential to good health both mentally and physically.

The world food processors, the drug companies and our governments are killing us with the things they allow us to eat and drink. They allow known poisons (things that our bodies do not recognize as food) into our food, water and our medicine supply. All in the name of giving you what you say you want. Some of the foods and medicines are necessary and others are questionable at best.

How do you tell them that you want these things? We tell them that we want these things with the items that you spend your money on, it's just that simple.

Do you want these practices to change? Read the ingredient list on the things you buy. Search on your computer or smart phone to see if any of them are bad for the human body or mind. Then don't buy that product if it has a known poison or even a questionable ingredient in it. They will stop making it if it does not sell and start making more healthy foods as they see your dollars going in that direction. They are simply chasing your dollars, spend them wisely. If enough people start making better choices in the grocery store then the system will be forced to change without so much as a harsh word.

You don't have to write a letter to your Congressman or complain to a company's deaf ears. Companies only listen to your purchasing and voting habits anyway. So, only buy what is actually good for you and only vote for politicians that are getting the job done that they were elected to do. They will listen to that and change the way they do things quickly.

Before our food supply was adulterated with ingredients that most other countries won't allow in their own food supplies, we did not have these problems at this rate per 1000 people. Prove it to yourself. Search the timeline of the US obesity rate and when it started to climb. Compare it to the different charts of proven harmful ingredients as they have been increasingly added to our food and drug supplies. Add in all the new fast foods and snack foods that have come available in those same years. Then compare the charts. They will almost parallel each other.

The handwriting is on the wall so to speak. Corporate profits are more important than your good health. If you don't believe it, search that as well, and read these reports; "Banned ingredients that are still legal in the US" and "the Top 10 scariest food additives", "the dirty dozen fruits and vegetables" and many others.

A great deal of the food in the grocery store has added sugar in it to make it more addictive so you will eat and buy more of it. They even use MRI machines to make sure their products have enough sugar, salt and fat in them to light up the same areas of the brain that cocaine does. That way they know you will become addicted to their products and they will have a constant customer, most times for life.

Companies produce a lot of toxic cleaners that they have made for us to clean our house with. On top of that are the toxic chemicals in toothpaste, make-up, deodorants and shampoos. Spend some time researching the products you put in and on your body. Can you stay away from all of them? Maybe not, but you can limit your exposure to them or handle them in a safer manner. All you have to do is make informed choices and not buy the harmful products and don't bring them into your home or use them on your body.

These things are just the tip of the iceberg. There are dozens of reliable reports like these on the Internet. Do some searching of your own about the products that you use and see what is in them. Do the math. We are eating, drinking and cleaning our homes, cleaning our mouths, bodies, scalp and hair with enough poison (I'm calling poison any ingredient that can harm your body) to make sure that you have some kind of health problem before you're an adult.

This is no conspiracy theory. These are just the facts. By purchasing their products we are telling manufacturers that we will let them put harmful chemicals into and on our bodies when we bring these products into our homes with our own purchases.

We are being poisoned for their profit and we are doing it to ourselves by not checking out what we are using in and on our bodies and bringing into our homes. Advertisements may be convincing, but as usual, it is buyer beware! They are all just fighting each other for your dollars.

All you have to do is *not* buy the products with questionable ingredients in them and they will quickly change the ingredients, or the products altogether so they can stay in business.

Now you know the ugly truth. What do you do from here? Simple, we have to get back to the basics. First, get the poisons and environmental toxins out of your life as much as possible. Go through your house and remove anything that has questionable ingredients in it or at least change the brand you buy next time and make sure that it is better for you. Get a water filter soon and learn how to use it.

Shop from the perimeter of the grocery store; then still be a smart shopper! That's where most of the real food is but even foods there need to be checked out carefully. Things such as cheap meats with fillers and meats from the animals that were fed GMO grains and pumped full of growth hormones, antibiotics and vaccines are not good for the body. You are getting these things in you as you eat these meats. The same thing is true with most dairy products unless these things are verified to be organic. Whatever they did to the cow is getting in you through the dairy products that you consume.

The middle of the grocery store is where most of the man made things are like bagged, boxed, canned, packaged, processed and bottled foods. These are the products that have the most man-made ingredients and preservatives in them. Make sure they are organic if you can afford them or at least limit how often you eat them if they are not.

At home eat fresh organic fruits, produce, organic dairy (if you can tolerate it), lean meats and seafood, that your body can tolerate. Drink plenty of the best filtered water that you can get. Then still be a smart shopper and read the ingredient list and only take home the safest products. Wash or rinse all fruits and vegetables before eating them. Learn which ones need to be peeled before eating them.

If you quit drinking sodas, eating the questionable snacks, smoking, and drinking too much alcohol then you will be able to afford the better foods and filtered water that will help to keep you in better health. As you quit these foods you will lose the addiction to them. If you don't want to quit some of these things then at least take a good long look at the effect they are having on your mind and body. Then ask yourself yet again if your health is worth the effort to stay away from them.

Research shows that we should drink plenty of clean water, and

even tap water in most places, is better for you than sodas and alcohol but filtered water is best. Doctors say that the beginning of
almost all disease is dehydration. So drink up and stay hydrated.
Sodas and alcohol dehydrate the human body.

Water rehydrates us and helps to flush the toxins out of our bodies. Low hydration concentrates the toxins and helps to bring on
inflammation and sickness.

Remember that a lot of people have food allergies and sensitivities. Don't eat things that give you painful indigestion, heartburn, upset stomach, a lot of gas or diarrhea! Those five things
and others are your stomach's way of telling you that those
foods are not good for you, listen to it. Some folks even get skin
rashes from certain foods or headaches and brain fog. Anything
like that after you eat something is your bodies way of telling
you to stop eating it.

Once again, by saving the money you used to spend on junk
food and other foods that your body doesn't seem to deal with
very well, it won't be long until you saved enough to buy a good
drinking water filter system that will take the most of the im-
purities out of the water that you are drinking. There are some
good low priced filtering pitchers out there, online and in stores,
get one if you can. It just makes good *Common Sense* to give yourself the cleanest water that you can get. Also get a water test kit
and be sure your water is PH balanced as the human body prefers
that. You can buy the PH kits and get PH balance drops online if
your water supply needs it.

Read about the studies that show that all kinds of prescription medicines are starting to show up in our drinking water. It's from being flushed down the toilets when they expire and they are getting into our groundwater. That means that we are drinking them and bathing in them as well. So, dispose of old medications properly. Most counties have days when you can take your old medications and vitamins to a safe place for disposal. Take the labels off the bottles. The only ones that need to know what medications you are on are you and your Doctor.

Now, read the older toothpaste tubes about the fluoride in toothpaste, because they changed the writing on some of the new ones. They tell you to call poison control if you actually swallow too much toothpaste. How do you brush your teeth without actually swallowing some of it? How much is too much. Does it accumulate and oh yes, fluoride is in the water you drink as well if you drink city water. There is no real proof that it is good for you and there are other countries that don't allow it in their water systems.

I'm not saying anything new here. Countries like Belgium, Germany and Sweden and others will not allow fluoride in their water. This information has been around for a long time. I'm just putting a lot of it in one place so you can get the big picture all at once.

I personally did not know the first person in school, in my neighborhood or town with cancer when I was growing up in the 50s and 60s. It's not that there weren't any, it's just that there wasn't that many of them nor were there as many obese children and adults.

It was only 1962 when St. Jude's Children's Hospital first opened its doors. That means we were just reaching a point where we had enough children in the country with cancer to need a Children's Hospital just for children with cancer.

Look at that timeline of obesity rates, disease rates and new cancers. You will find that the more sugars and processed foods, high powered prescriptions, manmade food additives and GMOs that were coming into our diets, the more problems we experienced. Also, there were not as many people around that were obese nor that had cancer before all these changes came into our diets. What does that tell you? It should tell you that something had really changed. A large part of it is the actual water that we drink, foods that we eat and medications that we take. Then there is the more polluted environment that we now live in as well. Air pollution is so bad in some places that it reduces visibility.

As usual, it is buyer beware. Choose the products that you bring into your home carefully. No one is making you buy these products. The only reason that you do so is because you don't read or understand the ingredients list. Maybe you fell for the advertisements for those products or the addictive flavors they created. Don't let *your* taste buds kill *you* by *your* own hand and by the things *you* paid for.

So grab some food out of your cabinets and do a search on the ingredients. Especially the ingredients that you don't know and do some research! Grab a pen and make a list of the ingredients you find that are questionable and take the list to the store next time you go shopping. Then, just don't buy anything with those ingredients in it. No matter how good you think it tastes. That's where they get you. They have made poison taste good and found out how to make it as addictive as cigarettes and cocaine and we fell for it.

Now about sugars, it is hard on the body in any variety when too much of it is eaten. Studies have shown that the body only needs about 25 to 40 grams of sugar a day, depending on whether you are a woman or a man and what size you are. You get that much in one can of most sodas. Can your body handle more sugar, of course it can especially when we are younger. Should you at least try to cut back and stay in a safer range? That is up to you. Bad choices *will* catch up to you as you age.

Have I always thought like this? No, I wasn't told these things as a child and a younger man. The foods were not as manipulated yet either. As I found these things out I learned better ways to care for my body. I have tried to act on that knowledge as much as possible. I have refined my diet constantly over the years as I found better ways to take care of it and better foods for it. I continue to modify my diet even today as I learn more about the foods that I am eating.

I just wish someone had told me these things a lot earlier. I would not have so much work to do to fix the damage that I have already done to my body.

Search for "the worst foods for your health", "The 10 worst foods that you can buy" and "15 reasons to kick sugar". Spend some time researching what you shouldn't eat and even more time researching what you should eat. Remember that the internet is filled with false information so verify what you find.

There are many studies on all subjects and someone will argue for or against anything. So always double check what you read and allow for a degree of doubt in almost all of them. Always check the source as well. If it is written by the company that makes it then it probably leans in their favor. Like a certain big poison maker claiming their products are safe. A lie repeated often enough can appear to become truth but it is still a lie.

The studies that I found on this subject show that sugar is metabolized in your liver. Your liver serves as the main glucose buffer, preventing high or low extremes of blood sugar. Your liver is the key regulator of blood sugar between meals due to the fact that it manufactures, stores and releases glycogen, the starch form of glucose. When your blood sugar is low, a healthy liver convert's stored glycogen into glucose, releasing it into the bloodstream to raise blood sugar levels. When your blood sugar is high, a healthy liver will convert the excess into stored glycogen or fat.

Fruit sugars are different than manmade sugars and they are processed differently by your body. The fiber in the fruit minimizes the sugars impact on blood sugar levels. You also get vitamins, minerals and other healthy nutrients from fruits. Healthy adults should eat about 1½ cups of fruit per day. Most fruit juices are slightly different as some still have the vitamins and minerals but they don't have the fiber of whole fruits and most have added sugar. This gets their sugars into your system much faster and juices have almost twice the calories and sugar compared to the whole fruit. Beware some fruit juices have very little real juice in them. Once again read the labels.

Also, your body needs a certain amount of healthy fats so don't try to totally eliminate healthy fats from your diet. Learn which healthy fats, like avocados and extra virgin olive oil etc, are good for you as well as which fats like vegetable oils that are bad for you. Remember, we are all different, learn what works best for *you* and your body.

Too much manmade sugar helps to create too much inflammation in the body. Inflammation is normal, but too much is not normal and it is not good for you. Add to that by not drinking enough water and letting your body become dehydrated and that creates another one of the leading causes of disease. The combination of dehydration and too much inflammation are two of the things that hurt our bodies most. Then add shallow breathing (instead of getting full breathes) or a lack of oxygen to that and disease comes on even faster.

So, at least don't bring products that have high sugar content into your home and be sparing with the ones that you do. Always read the serving size when you read the sugar content. They count on you thinking that the amount on the label is all that is in the package. If there are 10 servings in the package, there is 10 times that amount of sugar in the package that it says that it has per serving.

Health professionals are trying to make manmade sugar a controlled substance, like alcohol and tobacco, so they can get soda machines out of the schools. It's that hard on your body and they know it.

In the 1700s the average human only consumed about 4 pounds of sugar a year. By 1800 it was about 18 pounds per year. By 1900 it was 90 pounds per year. By 2009 50% of Americans consumed 180 pounds per year. In 2008 Americans consumed about 37.8 pounds of high fructose corn syrup per year. In 2008 the obesity rate reaches 32.2% for men and 35.5% for women and 400,000 die annually from obesity. Want to reconsider you love of sugar?

1906—A German physician, Dr. Alzheimer, first identifies a form of dementia characterized by dramatic shrinkage, (Sugar's Sordid Timeline History 21), in brain nerve cells. By the end of the 20th century, an estimated 5 million Americans a year will be diagnosed with Alzheimer's disease.

I wasn't really overweight at 5'7" and 165 pounds, and I've been that way for years. However, when I learned this about sugar, I decided to experiment. The only change I made was to take as much manmade sugar out of my diet as possible. My aim was to cut out at least half of the sugar that was currently in my diet and that was easy. I just compared labels until I found products of my liking with less sugar. By doing that, 10 pounds walked off my body in one week. Keep in mind that I am very physically active, but I made no other changes. I ate just as much food. I just changed what I ate.

Then I was diagnosed with silent reflux, which is acid reflux with no symptoms until you get a dry cough that won't go away. So, I went on a reflux friendly diet. I started eating more fresh fruits and lots of vegetables and plenty of good lean protein and increased my daily intake of water and healthy fats. I try to get only wild caught fish and other organic meats. Also, I occasionally eat local venison, which is very lean and organic, unless it has been eating genetically modified plants and corn!

One week after starting that change in my diet, that was also for the betterment of my health, my body dropped another 10 pounds in one week. So, now at 5'7" and 145 pounds, I feel better, and have more energy and my workouts are easier.

Remember, we are not only a representation of *what* we eat, but *what* our food eats as well. If the animals that we eat are eating harmful things or being injected with harmful chemicals, then we consume those things when we eat them. The same goes for our fruits and vegetables if they are sprayed with harmful herbicides and pesticides that stay in them after they are harvested. We are getting those poisons in us as well.

Almost all non organic grains are sprayed with Roundup to *brown* the harvest so the farmer doesn't lose about 10% of the harvest at the mill from not being mature or ripe. Do you really think all that poison is gone? It ends up in your breads, cereals, crackers, pasta and canned goods. Milk and dairy products have their own problems from all the vaccines, hormones and antibiotics that are put into the cows. You get that when you eat or drink any dairy product that is not organic.

The point is, be careful of what you bring into your home to eat and drink. Take care of the only body you will receive for this lifetime and it will respond wonderfully. It is an amazing healing machine, but it can't start healing until you stop putting the poisons and environmental toxins in it. By poisons, I mean anything that is not natural for the body to consume.

Remember yet again, the body was designed "before" the pharmacy and the grocery store with all its bagged, boxed, canned, processed, bottled and packaged foods. Most of them have added hormones, antibiotics, vaccines, preservatives, herbicide, pesticides, food colorings and artificial flavors and manmade sugars in them. The body needs good natural foods to be at its best. Do the math as the body can't take all this for too long before it just starts to give up. It's actually a slow painful form of suicide.

They claim that some of these things are necessary to grow enough food for all the people on this planet, but there are safer ways to use them and better preparation practices of the foods before you eat them. Learn which fruits and vegetables need peeling before you eat them and do so.

As if that is not enough, you need to learn about the packaging that your food is packaged in. If it is plastic lined cans, almost all of them leech BPAs out of the liner and into the foods in them unless they say that they are BPA free. BPAs are considered to be the new lead, as far as poisons are concerned.

Check out the packaging as well and **never microwave in plastic or the Styrofoam containers** that foods are packed and stored in. These things were never meant to be exposed to heat. **Never** store foods in the can they came in after they are opened if you didn't use all of the food in the can. Always put it in a proper food storage container.

Eat mostly, if not completely, what your body runs on the best. Go with as many fresh fruits and fresh vegetables along with clean dairy (if you can tolerate it). Buy lean meats, safe fish and other seafood, organic breads and pastas if you can. However, limit the breads and pastas as they are high in carbohydrates and too many carbohydrates are not good for your body. The food pyramid needs to be modified to show better how today's food affect our bodies. Most sites suggest 30% clean lean protein, 30% good healthy fats and 40% carbohydrates. Remember that most vegetables have good carbohydrates in them where as most breads and pastas do not. Some vegetables have high carbohydrates and some fruits are real high in sugar. It's *your* job to find what works best for *your* body.

Learn about food combining. There are many different theories on this so follow whatever works for you and even that will change as you age and your body changes. The basics of this are taught different by many nutritionists.

When we are young it seems that most folks can digest almost anything without many problems. As we age the digestive system has a harder time with improper food combinations that we try. Just look at all the antacids, acid reducers and acid reflux medications that are on the market. They are some of the top sellers to aid with digestion. This is only because we eat too many wrong combinations of food at the same meal or foods that don't agree with *our* stomachs. It is also because we eat some things that we have food sensitivities to. It's up to you to figure that out as you try different things.

If we learn how to properly combine good foods in the proper combinations and the right portion sizes during our meals, most of us will not need any of these medications to help us digest. It is also said to help digestion if we do not drink anything 30 minutes before we eat, during the meal and up to 30 minutes after the meal. This allows the liver, the pancreas and the gall-bladder to do their jobs without having to produce more acid and bile than they have to too help digest your food. The more you drink the more they have to produce to do the same job. Basically when you drink during a meal you are over working this part of your digestive system because you are diluting your stomach acids.

There are some foods that should not be eaten with other foods so that they will digest properly. For instance, they say that melons and some fruits should be eaten alone or left alone. The reason is that they digest quickly and are meant to be in the intestines in that short time period for your body to get the most benefit from them. If they stay in the stomach too long they will start to ferment.

It is said that proteins (meats) and starches (potatoes, bread, rice etc.) should not be combined because it is harder on the stomach to digest those combinations. Proteins should be eaten with vegetables. Starches should be eaten with vegetables. However, proteins and starches should be kept separate for most folks. Once again, whatever works best for your body as some folks always eat this way and have no visible problem at the time.

The question is; will it catch up to you in the future? If you eat this way and have to take a medication to help stop heartburn, indigestion, constipation or diarrhea then it is possible that changing the way you eat may stop the need for the medications. Most of these medications say not to stay on them for more than 2 weeks anyway. Read the literature that comes with the medication and make sure you are taking it correctly. Once again your body is constantly telling you what it needs if you will just listen.

Think about this, you go to a buffet and have a salad with many different things in it and covered with a sugary high calorie dressing. Then you hit the food bar and have some of several meats and multiple veggies and starches. Then you head for the dessert bar just to make sure that you got your money's worth and try several different deserts and top that off with iced tea, sodas or coffee. Then you wonder why your meal is sitting so heavy on your stomach and that you have to follow it up with some type of digestive medication. Don't get me wrong as some folks can eat like this as they just have that cast iron gut. Others can't eat this way without digestive problems. However if you have to take digestive meds just to eat then it may be time to change your eating habits. It's your health so it's your choice.

This is your stomachs way of telling you that it just can't keep trying to process that many different combinations of food. The reality of it is the KISS theory, **Keep It Simple Stupid**. For most people one protein and 3 vegetables are good. You might be able push it a little further by using say, 2 types of squash, 2 different colors of peppers, 2 types of cabbage, 2 types of onions or the same protein cooked in a couple of different ways. So making it interesting is still easy.

Just remember that most of our ancestors did not have large food choices or fully stocked grocery stores as recently as about 100 years ago. Hereditarily our digestive systems are not prepared for this many food choices. This helps to explain why so many are going to their doctor for digestive medications unnecessarily and gaining too much weight.

So try simple meals with clean fresh water for your drink (but not during the meal). Then give it a few months and see how your body responds. If you are having problems with your body in any way, a simple diet with proper food combining might just be all you need to make it better. You won't know if you don't try. Even then you need to allow enough time to see the change. Remember it took all the years that you are old to get this way and it will not change in a few weeks.

Again, about drinking "while we eat", our digestive system works best when our digestive acids are not diluted during the meal. Try not to drink 30 minutes before, during and 30 minutes after the meal to allow your stomach time to easily digest the food. Always chew your food well as digestion starts in the mouth. If you swallow food almost whole then the stomach has a lot more work to do to break down your food. Chewing your food well keeps from over working the pancreas and the gall bladder and the liver.

"You" are in charge of what and how you eat! So just change your diet to what's good for your body and watch it become healthier. Just don't forget to meditate and deep breathe. Drink enough clean water and get plenty of exercise.

You have been doing it your way all these years. If your body doesn't look and feel the way you want it to, it might just be time for a change of diet and exercise. What have you got to lose? You may just end up getting the good health that you have been wanting. When is a better time to start than now?

To finish this chapter I would like to share a personal experience as an example. I was eating what I "thought" was a healthy diet. Breakfast was eggs, bacon, grits or potatoes and wheat toast 1 day. Then oatmeal with some walnuts, pumpkin seeds and fruits the next day. Then full fat yogurt that is low in sugar with nuts, seeds and fruits 1 day and rotate these. Then a banana for a snack, lunch was a healthy salad or a Boars Head sub or a chicken quesadilla with salsa. The afternoon snack was an apple, or nuts and seeds, and a healthy dinner of lean protein, healthy fats and veggies.

On the days I would eat the yogurt with blueberries and such, I would get brain fog after I ate. I knew it had something to do with the food but yogurt had never done that to me before. So I started looking into it and decided to just take the yogurt out of my diet and that helped. My body changed as I got older. Or the product changed, I am not sure which one it was or even possibly both of them.

I finally found a blood test that uses your own blood to test it against 184 different foods on 2 different charts to see what other food sensitivities I might have. Turns out I am sensitive to almost all dairy/yogurt, blue berries, apples, bananas, almonds, pineapple, watermelon, green beans, mushrooms, crab, quinoa and gluten to name some of them. So my body was trying to tell me that some of these foods weren't great for me. Most of them are healthy foods, just not for me or that often. As you can see from the things I was eating, I was having reactions to what I was eating. I am also sensitive to almost all of the ingredients in beer and breads. They had to go out of my diet as well. After all, my best health is worth the change and there are still plenty of great foods out there for me to choose from and enjoy in moderation.

The blood tests are; IgG and IgA ELISA 184 food panels and I found out about them from a chiropractic-Internist. They aren't cheap but the info about how my food affects my body is priceless. It's an investment in your future health. Are they 100% correct, probably not but I will take that chance and hold off on anything I might be sensitive to in order to benefit my health. I can always add it back later. So far it is working well.

Always do your research, before you choose any new Dr. as some are better and more trained than others and some are just snake oil salesmen. As usual, it is buyer beware.

During this time I also learned about intermittent fasting. That means to eat dinner as early as you can, depending on your schedule. Shoot for about 12 hours between your dinner and your breakfast if you can with no night time snacking. This gives your digestive system a break to shut down and just relax. If you snack before bedtime you digest into the night while your body wants to shut down and sleep. Calorie restrictions can also help but that depends on what is going on with the rest of your diet and your body. Talk to your family Dr. first.

Something else to know about our food supply, it's not as healthy as it was even 10 years ago. The widespread use of herbicides, pesticides and antifungal sprays applied on our crops, combined with the antibiotics, vaccines, and hormones put into the livestock have increased. Along with the GMO corn, soy and Glyphosate sprayed grains that the animals are feed to eat, have made these animals breads, grains and vegetables less healthy for humans to eat.

If you want this practice to stop then just buy organic and they will chase your dollars by changing these practices. Simply buying these less healthy foods tells the food producers that you want them and they will continue these practices until you quit buying the crap.

Our soils are more polluted and depleted of quality minerals than ever before. The water they use to grow them with is more polluted as well. Our plants no longer give us all the vitamins and minerals that they should be giving us because of that. It is estimated that it takes more than double the amount of vegetables to get the same vitamin and mineral content from your food as it did in the past.

Add into that mix all the additives in our foods, like MSG, artificial sweeteners, artificial flavors, high fructose corn syrup, trans-fats, food dyes, sodium nitrate and nitrite, potassium bromate, and the list goes on and on. Add to that the more polluted that our water and air is and you start to see why some people are in the shape they are. These things weren't in our foods before the obesity and cancer epidemic that we are seeing now. Take them out of your diet and start to heal. The more natural your food and water supply is, the better your health will be.

Use *Common Sense* in the grocery store and don't fall for the advertisements or the addictive tastes. Oh, and now they are finding glyphosate/Roundup in children's cereals, some fruits and vegetables, breads, oatmeal and in some beers and wines. It is turning up in some municipal water supplies from runoff from cow, pig and chicken farms, plant farms, nurseries and golf courses. You get another possible problem with your water if you are downstream from a nuclear plant. Educate yourself about your food and drink and become a smart shopper and be careful out there.   Life is supposed to be good, healthy and fun.

Let's get that back if you have lost it.

CHAPTER 12
OUR CHOSEN
POISONS

Regardless what it is, if you are putting it in or on your body or spending your money on it, you should ask yourself; is this good for my body and my financial future or is it hurting them? Do you want your life, health, finances or your life situation to improve? If the answer to the second question is "no", then you might as well stop reading this chapter. If the answer is "yes", then these things might help you. Always remember that these are just suggestions as *you* must make the decision for what works in your life. I will remind you of this again at the end of this chapter and in several places in the book.

Now that you say that you want to improve then it is time to take a good long look at everything that you eat, drink, use in and on your body and everything that you spend your money on. Yes, I am constantly working on all of these things myself as my life, my health and my body is constantly changing as well. Every time I think I have it where it needs to be, life throws something else at me and I have to adjust my direction again.

Change is as natural as it is necessary yet we have to want it and allow for it daily. This is life's way of keeping us on our toes. Don't get me wrong if you like where you are and want no change that is your choice.

First understand that you have to really *want* the change that you are considering. A lot of people say they want better health or control over their finances or whatever else they may want to change in their life. However if they are not willing to make the change in their food choices, their spending habits and their daily activities to accomplish that change then it will not happen on its own. You can't create the change you want using the same actions that got you where you are.

If you are determined to make changes for the better then make a list of everything that you put into your body. No matter how it goes in your body whether you, eat it, drink it, shoot it, smoke it, snort it or ingest it in any manner.

Make another list of everything that you put on your body. Lotions, potions, perfume, too much sun, harmful chemicals from cleaning, work related situations or anything! Now, make two columns to the right of your lists. Label these columns, "Good for the human body" and "Bad or probably bad for the human body". These lists can be on paper or mental but paper gives you something to look at daily.

Search for and research each thing. Each item will usually fall into one of these two columns. There are very few things that will end up in a grey area. If it's bad for you, it's probably holding you back or hurting your body. If you quit these poisons and spending habits, that can be money you can use towards getting the better food, life, or health that you want. It is money that you can save for the things you really want and need or for your future or retirement.

Now ask yourself again just how bad that you want improvement in any of these areas of your life mentally, physically or financially etc. What on your list appears to be holding you back? A better question is; will you make the necessary changes in your list to get the health and the life that you say that you want. Are your bad spending and eating habits, mild food addictions and your sweet tooth worth more to you than your good health, a bigger bank account and a better future? This is *your choice* so make it count. There is no wrong answer as you must decide the direction you want your life to take.

Is it peer pressure holding you back from the changes you want? People that always want you to share in where they are going, what they are eating, drinking, smoking etc.? Spend less time with anyone like that even if it means more time alone. Being alone can be really good if you use it properly. Try deep breathing, meditation, listening to the great self help teachers on YouTube. Start listening to your favorite music, walk in nature, take a road trip or enjoy petting your animal. Experiment with something that makes you feel good and will guide you in the right direction that you want to grow into.

If you have found that certain foods hold weight on you or make you feel bad then eliminate them. If someone insists that you try any of them, just tell them that you are allergic to those foods or products. Just be honest and they should leave you alone about it.

Maybe a change in you will bring about a change in them. You are what you eat! The choice is yours, not someone else's. Be the best you that you can be if that is what you want. You only get one body and one chance to get your body through this life. Make the best of it. Why not? What have you got to lose? Better yet, what will you gain? Just remember there are no promises in life so just make sure you truly want the change you are considering. Watch what you wish for as it just might happen.

If you find the things that are hurting you and holding you back, why would you not want to do your best to correct them? It's usually no harder to fix most of them than it was to create them. Sometimes less, sometimes more!

If you have been smoking for a long time, you may be able to stop in a day but remember that it may take a while to heal from the damage. But, no matter how long it takes it is always worth it.

If you are overweight and you have been eating foods that put that weight on you for a long time and you stop eating those foods all at once, it's still going to take a while to lose the weight. Be patient, it will be worth it.

If you have an addiction you can stop putting the poison in or on your body however it will take a while to heal from it. Be patient, the body is an amazing healing machine when you quit putting poison in or on it. However it helps a lot to do it before the stroke, heart attack or the sickness even starts.

No matter what you think, if you are doing something that hurts the mind, body or spirit, then you are heading for a brick wall that you just haven't looked up from your perceived fun to see yet. It's still there and coming at you. The sooner that you look up to see it, the easier it will be to change your actions.

You didn't get unhealthy overnight, so allow your body plenty of time to heal from all the damage that you have done to it. Better yet! If you are really young and have not really developed any really bad habits, concentrate on keeping it that way.

Are your bad habits worth your health, your money, your happiness or your life? Once again that choice is yours alone to make.

Just don't use the crutch phrase; "I can't do it". Because whether you say that you can or whether you say that you can't, either way you will prove yourself right.

Remember, clean water, foods that are good for your body, exercise, meditation, deep breathing and plenty of good restful sleep will go a long way to help us stay well. This is repeated yet again on purpose. It's to help drive the point home and help you remember it. Also get out into nature and get regular sunshine and fresh air.

Grounding is helpful and that is what the indigenous peoples and Native Americans practiced. Many folks today use it as well. It is simply going barefoot on the ground, the grass or the beach or getting into an ocean, river or a lake. This helps to *ground* your body to the earth and discharge negative magnetic energy that we pick up from computers, cell phones, power lines, cars, TVs etc. Once again, read up on the subjects that can improve your health. I say that because this book is meant to point you in a direction you might want to go. It is in your going down your own path and learning what you want to know that will teach you much better than my explanations. I'm just another messenger praying that my words will help another human find their favorite path sooner.

If we really want improvement, usually the only thing that is holding us back is ourselves. The answers are always within us, just keep looking deeper. Ask for help or make a search engine one of your new best friends and always check your sources. Even then, monitor how these changes affect you and be ready to adjust as needed.

Once again these are just my thoughts and opinions and they are only meant to give you food for thought as the end decision must be your own. Think long and hard on the changes you say you want. Think them as far through as you can and be ready to adjust as you see fit or even just stop and take time to review your progress.

There is a picture online of a little boy (about 6) in an attic play-room setting and it's called; the Journey Begins by Daniel Lieske. It is worth your time to look it up if you have the spirit of a child still in you.

The young man is on his knees with a backpack on and it has his teddy bear hanging out of it. He has a wooden sword in one hand and a ball of twine in the other that is tied to a post in the attic. This is so he can find his way home. He is looking into a magic mirror that has a winding road leading to a castle and a city. Around him are many fascinating items and his cat is be-hind him. He is contemplating his journey and what he will find in the city and the castle. Under the picture the artist has a full explanation of the artwork.

We are all on a journey called life. You might enjoy yours more if you take care of the body, mind and spirit that you are using to get you through it. Life is meant to be enjoyed, please enjoy your journey!

May the inner child in all of us live forever! I must admit that my inner child got pushed aside at a very early age and now in my mid 60s I am doing all I can to reconnect with him. Do your best to stay in touch with yours. Refuse to *completely* grow up. We need the inner child in us to stay with us through life.

CHAPTER 13
PERSONAL RELATIONSHIPS WITH OURSELVES AND OTHERS

The topic of personal relationships usually keeps me on my toes and honestly most of the other topics do too as my life circumstances continue to change. I don't immediately see the changes that I need to make so I keep looking deeper. I still have areas that I am working on because life keeps changing. I'm human, but I'm trying harder everyday to improve. I believe that is the key. Remember that the reason relationships are constantly changing is that we and all the others around us are all growing in different directions a lot of the time.

Sometimes I feel almost too logical around some people and then not logical enough around others. That makes me feel like I have come a good way in this life, but it also shows me that I have a lot more to learn. I plan to always be motivated and look for better ways to improve my life and circumstances.

As humans, we are constantly changing and growing in different ways. It is part of our nature. We achieve something and almost immediately we start to look for what is next on our list.

All through life most of the people we meet come and go. One day we think that we have met our new best friend and later in life we look back and wonder where they are now. If we are fortunate enough, some of them will stay with us along our journey for a lifetime.

Some people are with us long enough to help teach us things that helped to shape us in the direction we seem to be going. Some teach us what we don't want to be like and others teach us what we do want to be like. Some folks come along just to show us a new direction or to teach another one of life's infinite lessons. If we are lucky we find someone that wants to share the journey.

Seeing a family member, friend or loved one stuck going down a road that you know is not beneficial for them is hard to watch. We want to share a potential better way for them to consider. However I am learning that it is best to just accept where different people are in their life and where I am in mine. Then either enjoy their company the way they are, or simply move on. Trying to change people to the way we think is best for them to be doesn't work. That being said, if a friend is asking for help and you can share that help then by all means help them.

We can only change ourselves. However, we can show others by our own actions that there is another way. Patiently planting the seed of, there is a different way, seems to be better than demanding someone change because we think that what they are doing is wrong. This happens a lot in relationships and even though we might not be able to see their path, it might not be wrong for them at that time. Who knows, maybe the way we are thinking is not completely right for them or us. This is where inner reflection helps as most of us only change when we decide to anyway.

It is best for you to always stand up for yourself or for what is right when whatever someone else is doing is hurting you or just leave if you can. If someone is giving you a hard time or taking advantage of you, your family or friends by demanding that you do things their way, then ask them to please stop. If they will not stop then don't get around them if you do not have to or limit that time as much as possible.

There are some people that want to change so quickly that they will listen to someone else who already is where they think they want to be. The key here is simply that like attracts like. If you hang out with and emulate someone that is already where you want to be, you just might catch a break and get there faster. It works but you still have to put in the effort to change and do it in a way that works right for you.

One of my biggest pet peeves, and so it is with most of the people that I know, are the people that don't ask us if we *want* to do something that they have planned. They just *assume* we do and call to tell us our part in *their* plans. Then they actually just expect us to do what they want done. Unless you are paying me or I have an obligation to you then I have the right to decide if I want to do what you have asked. If you really do not want to do something, then say so up front. Do not let anyone talk you into anything you do not want to do.

Really we should ask the other people in our plans if they even want to be a part of our plans in the first place and give them the right to say no. It is called co-creation and it makes a lot of sense. There is no wrong answer when you ask someone if they want to be part of your plans. Everyone has the right to their own opinion.

There are times when someone you know will say that they want something specific yet their actions seem to be going the opposite way. All you can do is point that out and if they want to stay on their current path then you must let them do so. You can lead a horse to water but you can't make him drink. Depending on who that is in your life, you may have to just move on and let them be until they see and want the actual change they claim to want. I think we are all guilty of this on some subject at different points in our lives. I know that I am.

If you say that you want to live a healthier life and you open the 2nd pack of cigarettes for the day or you say that you want to get sober while they are opening the 6th beer for the night or lose weight while eating yet another bad for the body food choice, well I hope you get the point here. Here is the key to my point. Your actions need to match your words, at least most of the time, especially if you are asking someone else to help you with your situation.

There are many wonderful teachers on subjects that teach better ways to live. Esther Hicks, Mike Dooley, Alan Watts, José Silva, Edward Cayce, Anthony Robbins, Will Smith, Wayne Dyer, Joseph Weed and many others are worthy of your attention. You can even look further back to earlier teachers like Earl Nightingale, Napoleon Hill, Thomas Paine and many more, they are all very inspiring. I encourage you to search for all of them and any other teachers that you feel a connection with. We all hear things differently and connect with different people on various subjects as we go through life.

Most of these teachers have their own websites and I encourage you to find them and spend time listening to the ones that you connect with. A lot of their information is available online and on YouTube and other sites like it. You can also get some of their books and read them at your leisure.

I offer a lot of my content on my Face Book and Twitter pages for free. The links are in this book. YouTube is a wonderful site for getting free self help. I tip my hat to the other people that offer information like this for free. It is priceless. Spend some time each day with some of the wonderful teachers you will find and others that you will find along your way. The time you spend with them will be priceless.

Make good use of your Internet time. Try to reach out in new directions instead of listening to the same reruns on radio and TV stations or social media. Do not watch the news all day because as you should have come to notice that most of it is designed to keep you stressed out. Just glance at headlines if you must and don't read completely negative stories. It is extremely rare that we would be able to fix those problems anyway. Broaden your mind reading good and happy news. Stretch yourself out in new positive directions. Life is best when we are enjoying it. I know, sometimes bad stuff happens to almost all of us. Just do your best to make your way through it.

To start going in a better direction try yoga, deep breathing exercises and meditation. Go for a walk, go ride a bike, get physical exercise and just enjoy being outdoors when you can. Call or visit a friend or family member. Go see a good movie or watch something enlightening or funny on YouTube or something new or about nature on TV. If you allow your mind to go in these directions as well as in your day-to-day life, you will never again be bored. If you get bored, you are letting yourself down. There is so much free stuff to do and see nowadays, that there is no excuse to be bored unless you just want to be. And then you can always work on your personal to do list if you can think of nothing else to do or take a good nap.

There is a lot to be said about taking some time to quiet your mind and meditate. Just turn off all other thoughts and focus on your breathing. Search the word "meditation" on YouTube or your favorite search engine and find the type that you enjoy and do it at least 15 minutes a day. Meditation helps to bring about personal growth. That alone will help you with all of your other relationships and situations.

You will not get along with all of your friends, family members or coworkers all of the time. It just isn't that possible. Usually it is because of a difference of opinion or someone just trying to push your buttons. Yes, there are some people that enjoy watching you blow up and get mad over nothing more than their words. Don't fall for it. Laugh at them and move on. If they continue you may want to limit your time with them.

So let's think about other people's words.

Unless you are dealing with authority figures or people in charge of your well being or even a boss, remember this, they can only upset you with their words if you take those words personally.

Other than that it is just their opinion. And that is all the words are, just an opinion. If you are in a casual conversation and someone expresses an opinion that you don't care for, it does not mean that you have to take their words to heart. Don't think of it as if it is something that they expect you to believe or do. Again, unless they are your parents, your boss or an authority figure that is in charge and they are asking you to do things you need to be doing and that won't hurt you. Even if they do expect you to do what they suggest it is still up to you to decide if that is the direction that you want to go. Once again, unless they are in charge and it is in the best interest of all and won't hurt you.

We get too caught up in all the "he said, she said" crap anyway. All anyone's words are is just their opinion of the matter. As long as they are not trying to force that opinion on you, then just let them have their opinion while you keep yours and walk away. Once again, unless it is your boss, parents or law enforcement,

the IRS etc. you hopefully get the point. If the judge says this is what you will do, you just might want to pay attention.

If your friends ask you to quit doing something that they don't like or ask you to do something that you don't care to do, you might want to get their perspective on it and ask; 'why'? In the end it is still your choice. This does not apply unless you are hurting someone or about to do something really stupid. Once again, someone's words in a casual conversation or even in an argument are just an opinion. Let them have it because they will defend it. Then if you try to force your opinion on them you will only end up in a more heated argument. Remember there are folks that like heated arguments and go out of their way to start them. You may want to limit your time with them as well.

Choose your friends wisely based on loyalty, respect and appreciation for each other. Then it helps for the friendship to have honesty, integrity and a genuine good feeling for each other. The more positive qualities you can find in someone the better that relationship can be.

I'll repeat this again because it fits here as well. The subject of Human Relations was only taught to me after high school in the tech school setting. It should be taught in the home and grade school, with refresher courses in middle school and high school as well. This can help to bring kids to a better understanding of the actions of others. It will also help them to better understand their own actions, feelings, and emotions and at a much younger age and throughout the rest of their life.

How much better could our society be, if we were taught the basics of human wants, needs, desires, interactions and actions at an early age? Then reinforce that knowledge all through our growing years into adulthood and teach it to our children and grand children.

We probably wouldn't be seeing near as much anxiety, hate, greed, jealousy, fear and mental issues from simple and unnecessary misunderstandings between people. Especially over simple opinions that come out of people's mouths. How much happier could we be if we just left someone else's opinion where we heard it. If we don't agree with it we can always leave it with them where it usually belongs.

Hearing other people's opinions should be no more than a sounding board of thoughts for us to sift through, so we can fine tune our own thoughts. I like this thought and will try it, but I'm not too sure about that thought, so I'll just think about it. That thought is just too far out there for me to consider at this time. I might be able to consider it again in the future, if it makes better sense then.

Always be open to new learning experiences and new ways to think about everything. Never think that just because you found a way that works for you now, that it is the only way or even the best way. There is almost always a better way to do most things than the first way that we find. This will keep your mind open to positive ways to move forward in your life. Everything in life changes so change with it as soon as you can.

One area that people tend to use as a social crutch is the phrase "I am sorry". If people are truly sorry, that means that they realize that they did something wrong and that they won't do it again, especially to the same person. To continue to do the same thing, over and over again and only apologize for it, means they don't really care. They are just going through the motions to smooth over the hurt that they have constantly caused another so that they can continue to do it. Once again limit your time with people like this or just move on and make better friends.

Saying you are sorry only to go do the same thing again is kind of like going to church to just to ask forgiveness for what you did last week. Then you think that you can go back out there and do it yet again next week with a clean slate, only in your own mind of course.

In reality, if you have hurt someone or screwed something up, *Common Sense* says that only saying that you are sorry will not fix what you broke or help the person that you hurt feel much better. You need to go the extra mile and actually fix the problem that you caused and stop doing anything that you have to continue to say; I'm sorry for.

In our dealings with others, if we would just take a minute to think about our words before we let them out of our mouths, (yes, I still struggle with this one as well) we could eliminate a lot of hard feelings and misunderstandings. That being said, if someone looks at us and speaks the absolute truth and we find ourselves upset or offended, it might just be time to look in the mirror and think about changing what seems to upset us about ourselves. It happens to me when I least expect it.

Let's speak of our actions. I am a believer in paying it forward, as in, when someone that we don't know or won't see again helps us. Just do something as good or as good as you can, in the near future, and help someone else.

I am also a firm believer in paying it back. If someone goes out of their way to help me, I am definitely be going to go out of my way to help them. Hopefully with things that are just as important to them and I will do it soon after they have helped me. Remember to always show proper appreciation for their help at the time when they help you. A heartfelt thank you goes a long way. Too many people *allow* someone to help them and move on without even a thank you. If you *allow* someone to help you it is no different than if you had *asked* them for help.

We should all remember that we get ahead with each other's help. None of us got where we are completely on our own. We all had help along the way. So always try to be there for those that have been there for you. If you make it to the top then reach down and help another person on their way up. That is the purpose of this book. Help the ones you love and every now and then lend a hand to a stranger (in a safe environment of course).

We should hold no one back. We should help almost everyone get ahead if we can. This doesn't mean that you should do without for yourself or continue to help someone that doesn't care. Don't give away your own vital resources that keep you alive. Unless extreme circumstances compel you to do so! Give from your excess as you can, not from your own core needs. You can't help others as well if you are lacking the same thing that you are giving.

Your help for others can be time helping a friend, a shoulder to cry on or an ear to vent to. You can give cash if you have it and that feels right to you. Anything that fits the occasion! Once again, this is unless you don't really have enough of these things for yourself! Always remember to say thank you for any help that you are given and show heartfelt appreciation to those that give help to you.

Personal relationships and intimate relationships can become so close that parting can cause heartbreak. While some heartbreak cannot be avoided some of it can pass quicker just by simply understanding basic human relations. People either grow together or they grow apart and this is natural so sometimes you just have to let go. There are many types of heartbreak and I will share a few with you for understanding what I mean.

Before my father left when I was around 5, it would break my heart for him to hit me more and harder than the situation called for. First I did not understand and second he would never explain, he would just lash out. It also broke my heart when he left even though we were not close because for better or worse he was the father figure in my life.

My next real heartbreak was when Mom had to work 2 jobs a day to be able to take care of us. I had to become a ward of the state and had to live in a children's home during 1st, 2nd and 3rd grade while my Mother worked until she could afford a house for us to live in. Not being able to live with your Mom at that age was hard to understand. We moved a lot and having to leave newly made friends and start over in new schools on a regular basis was hard as well.

The next time was when one of my first girlfriends cheated on me and left me for another guy. I thought we were in love but evidently she wasn't. Thank God she left as I can see now it was a good thing, even if it did crush me when it happened. I was beside myself for awhile because no one ever told me these things were going to happen. This happened with another girl friend later in life as well and I still let it hit me too hard and should have known better the second time.

The next time was when I got divorced and was only allowed to see my daughter every other weekend. Not being able to see her and hold her everyday was one of the biggest heartbreaks of my life. On those weekends I made sure that it was just her and I doing what she enjoyed the most even if it was just watching cartoons, playing games, watching a movie, going to the beach or visiting friends.

Then my next older brother died at 49 from cancer and I helped him till the end. It hurt me a lot when he died right in front of me while I held his hand. We had tried everything we could to help him beat it but it was stage 4 when they found it so I shut down my business to spend as much time with him as possible knowing he was going to pass.

There were smaller heart breaks along the way as people I thought were my friends changed and left but that was necessary for my growth as well. It was just hard to make sense of it at the time.

A really hard one for me was when my dermatologist called me and told me my test results showed that I had melanoma and might only have a year to live. I was only 52 and told him to cut out more than he thought might be needed to get it all and thank God it worked. I'm still alive and I'm 68. The heartbreak of thinking you are dying is a tough one as well.

The last real heart break to date was when my loving Mother got cancer and we went through that all over again. We spent as many of her remaining days with her as possible hanging out with her on the porch, having meals with her, taking her for treatments and to her Doctors appointments and anything else that she needed to have done for or with her to make it easier on her.

Seeing her heartbreak when we had to take her out of her home and put her in a senior care facility was a different kind of heartbreak. It was a helpless feeling.

I tell you these things so if they should ever happen to you that you will see that you will survive them. These things will either make you or break you, the choice is actually yours. Just keep doing the best that you can everyday and keep moving forwards. As long as you breathe there is life and what you make of that life is your choice. You can choose to be happy or sad at any time. Your circumstances will always be changing so take a deep breath and try your best to make sense of what is happening to you.

CHAPTER 14
PERSONAL
RELATIONSHIPS
WITH YOUR
SIGNIFICANT OTHER

First, both people should *want* to be together, you'd be surprised how many don't and still stay together. If you are in a relationship then the other person should get the bulk of your love and affection. Unless you have six kids, then there is not as much to go around. Still the other person should get the benefit of the doubt and consistent affection, if they want it. They should get your sincere appreciation and gratitude as well.

In a relationship, if you really care about and love each other and want to be together then there are some really basic rules. Do not lie, cheat or steal from each other. Do not be verbally or physically abusive. Give each other the benefit of the doubt. Spend quality time with each other, smile, laugh and enjoy your time together. If you are not doing these things, I must ask you, why are you still together?

Both people's needs should be met as much as possible. The alpha personality in the relationship should make sure that if their needs are getting met, so is the other persons. It's unfair when the alpha personality gets everything they want and their significant other barely gets what they need. You are both in this together because you choose to be, so be a team and see how far you can go. For God's sake be fair.

I am by no means a relationship specialist. However after many years of my own relationships, watching other relationships (both good one and rocky ones) and listening to people praise or complain or whine and cry about each other, I've got a fair grip on a good bit of it. Most of us do or have done these things but it hurts the relationship. The sooner we stop the better. Be fair with each other and always show kindness and love for your partner as much as possible. Almost all relationships are imperfect, including the ones I have been in. You either grow together or you grow apart.

A lot of this is caused by social conditioning. That is anything you have seen, been exposed to or endured so long that you have accepted it as ok when indeed it is not.

I am single right now because am looking for someone whom

even in our differences, we can find agreement or at least tolerance. In our worst argument, we can still have compassion and allow the other to have their opinion. No matter what we ask of the other we will always give as much back as much as we allow them to give to us. This includes anything that we *allow* the other to do *for* us as it must never be taken for granted. There is no difference between asking and allowing because you are receiving help either way. You get the benefit so show appreciation for it.

I have yet to have a relationship where the person gives back as much as they take from it or allow to be given to them. Your partner should allow you to be you as long as you aren't hurting them or anyone else or yourself. You should both agree to be able to disagree without either of you being wrong for your belief. That is unless your belief *is* wrong, such as abusing the other and feeling justified in doing so. If either person refuses to keep the relationship fair and moving forward, that is grounds for the other person to move on without hard feelings.

You can tell when you are giving the other person in your relationship what they want and need. They will always smile when you walk into the room. That is if there is no drama going on at the moment. And really it should go both ways. You know the love is still there if you both smile, when you see each other after a brief absence or even just at the end of the day. Especially if you both can relate to each other, listen to each other's day without criticizing and just always be there for each other at least most of the time.

You almost can't have an adult relationship without intimacy, or at least I can't. And from what I have seen, if you both aren't intimately compatible there will always be conflict in that area. Most of these relationships will not last, unless the other person can't get the courage to leave you. For one person will always be frustrated in that situation. However, there are people that live together just to share expenses but I am talking about relationships here.

Let me remind the reader yet again. I do not claim to have all the answers, probably not even most of them. These thoughts may only work for me and there are many better wordsmiths out there than me to write about these subjects. However, I'm way ahead of the guy that robbed the bank with the stickup note written on the back of his own deposit slip. And there seems to be quite a few like that out there. Just listen to the radio shows that have the "dumb crook news" and you will see what I mean.

I just don't see a lot of really basic *Common Sense* info for really young folks out there. Especially for children and those that haven't woken up one day with the thought that there just has to be more to life than just living day to day. I'm not saying that is wrong if that is exactly what you want out of life. We are all entitled to live any kind of life that we can create, from rich to poor or start with either and go either direction. Sometimes a more stress free life in the country is better for some folks. Then city life is better for others, while a life at sea suits some and anything else that you can imagine. It's your life so just how do you want to live it and on whose terms?

The point here is that we can all wake up *if* we want to. There are degrees to "waking up" and I still have a ways to go. Some are born awake, some have not started to wake up yet and others are completely enlightened. If more humans begin to "wake up" there will be much less chaos in the *world* and less suffering for many humans.

Let's get back to the golden rule, do onto others as you would have them do unto you. I'm starting to wonder if some people even remember it anymore. Then there are others that I wonder if they have ever even heard of it. Bring it back and share it with everyone.

There is enough love, energy and happiness to go around for everyone. All we have to do is make sure that we are fair in our dealings with others. Yes, it can be and is just that simple. Look around you. If you are demanding and getting most of what you want in your relationships with other people, and they aren't smiling and happy as well as you at the end of the day, then there is a damn good chance that you aren't being fair. If you aren't going to be fair in your relationship, expect the other person to leave you or at least give you the same crap back or ignore you. Everyone deserves equal happiness in a personal and intimate relationship.

Basically, in your relationships, don't pick on the other persons weakness or shortcomings unless they are pressing them on you. Then by all means speak up for yourself or move on. If you have been with someone awhile and always accepted certain traits and parts of their life and the way they do things as ok then keep doing so if you wish or if you have grown weary of it then say so and move on. Once again, humans either grow together or they grow apart. Let other humans out of your life as easy as you let them in your life and with no hard feelings. If it is meant to be you will grow back together.

It is usually a sign that someone is done with you when they start picking on you for the way you have always been or the way you have always done things since you met. Then there is the case where they thought they could change you and found out that they couldn't and now they are not happy about it.

In some cases your partner may have met someone else and they are looking to make the situation just bad enough to justify ending the relationship by picking on your flaws. They will usually blame it on you while they are doing it. This is a sign to just let them go. Walk away because it is better to be alone and a little lonely than being in a room with someone that is not happy with you for the way you have evolved since you met. That is unless you have gone over the deep end and changed for the worse or promised to change certain things and never followed through. I have seen it go both ways.

A good relationship starts with good, honest communication. Speak up early and constantly in all relationships. Think about your feelings and tell your partner if you feel like you are not being treated fairly and why.

If you do not like the way your partner is treating you, don't complain about it, just state your point and then listen closely to what they have to say about it. If the other person refuses to listen, then they probably never will and you need to decide right then if you want to continue to be in that relationship. Keep this in mind. In a fair relationship, you will never be asked to do any more than the other person is willing to give back.

Think about it. If you are doing things that your friends and family do not like, yet for whatever reason, they tolerate it, you will probably keep doing it. If you do things that they do not like and they don't tolerate it and walk away and quit associating with you, it will leave you with only a few choices. Stop doing it and apologize and hope they accept that or keep doing it and be alone or the possibility that you will be reprimanded for continuing to do it.

Remember, "human beings **will *always* make time** for what they truly want to do". If they promise to do things and never follow through and always have an excuse to not do them, then they never intended to in the first place. If they tell you that they would like to spend more time with you and never make that time, then they are just telling you what they want you to hear. Don't believe it, move on. Their actions speak the real truth so watch what they do, not what they say. Actions always speak louder than words anyway.

CHAPTER 15
GOOD MANNERS

I would like to finish the book with one of the most important character traits any human can have. Good Manners

A dictionary version: The treatment of other people with courtesy and politeness.

Along with *Common Sense* and a basic understanding of Human Relations the next most important things any of us can learn is Good Manners and Respect. Good Manners and Respect will help you weave your way through life a lot easier because people are drawn to other people with Good Manners that have Respect for them self and others.

Good manners go way beyond yes ma'am, yes sir, please and thank you. Holding a door for the person behind you regardless who it is, helping another that clearly is over burdened and you can see that they need a hand. Always being there for a neighbor, family member or friend in need, whether it is to help with a project, share a laugh or a smile, or to be an open ear or a shoulder to cry on. This list is endless.

Have respect not just for your parents and your elders but everyone you meet including yourself, unless they show no respect for you. Then take the high road and just smile and say; excuse me, I have to go now and move on. Lowering yourself to that level will only bring you down to a place you do not want to be.

Yes, it is hard to always take the high road and sometimes in the human experience you will find it to be impossible. In the case of war or just self defense, you must do what you have to do to survive. Be thankful that is not an everyday occurrence for most humans. This is part of what it is to be human in the first place. Try your best and always work on your faults but find forgiveness for yourself and the others you meet along the way.

Some older humans will almost always struggle with most of the topics in this book, as I know that I still do. That struggle may come from a lifetime of social conditioning that did not teach or demonstrate *Common Sense* or basic human relations at an early age to begin with. The bulk of the rest of our struggles are from our *ego* that jumps out at all the wrong times. Those who want to know even more about these things will look behind the curtain and see the truth.

We have a long world history of social conditioning that comes from greed, war, power and corruption that have created our current state of being. All of that along with public schooling that does not reflect all of the current needs of our young children. Add to that the households that do not provide enough adult guidance towards being the best human being a young person can grow up to be. All of these things have contributed to the lack of moral responsibility and the lack of good manners in so many ways that we see today. Each of us needs to always be a work in progress, getting better every day in any way that we can.

Here are some widely accepted dictionary versions of good manners that are in the public domain.

Good manners are an important thing to have since it shows that you're courteous to other people. Having good social etiquette can help you develop better relationships and make you more enjoyable to be around. If you're having a meal with others, then make sure you use good manners while you're eating to show that you're respectful. You also should maintain etiquette while you're online so you don't offend or over share with others.

Since part of this book is to get you using the internet and books to find great information instead of just hanging out on social media all night or watching videos TV reruns and playing the same old games. I encourage you to look up, good manners, and do some research on the subject as well as the other subjects in this book. This will also show you that it is more than just one human opinion on these subjects.

If you are fortunate enough in this life to make friends with someone that shares many of the things in life that you enjoy and they show and teach you new things of your benefit and show you love. Then be smart enough to give back as much as you can to show the same to them. Also do your best not to pick on things you do not yet understand about them.

Remember that God does not punish us. We punish ourselves by not being the best human beings that we can be. God just gives you the free will to experience your life anyway you choose. We just need to be taught how to make better choices in early childhood and be reminded that we are limitless human beings. The old ways of social conditioning children is what has us where we are. How many truly spend quality time teaching their young children Common Sense, human relations, meditation, deep breathing, and all the other things I speak about in this book. Common Sense, Love, Respect and Honesty needs to be prevalent in our society, schools and families. This is all my humble opinion and no one else needs to see this the exact same way. But I wish I had all this content taught to me in the 1950s as a child by well meaning family, caring friends and adults.

CONCLUSION

So now you are wondering about how more *Common Sense* thinking can improve your life and the outcomes of your actions. This is a good thing, think about it often, meditate on it and talk to your friends about using it more often and helping each other find better ways to get the best outcome to the things that confront you and them.

Sometimes we just need a fresh outlook to either guide us in a better direction or to confirm to ourselves that we are indeed on the right track to achieve our goals. One of the main keys to it is to always be willing to be flexible as things change. Always be ready to adjust your plans as necessary to keep your life momentum moving forwards. Try to keep mostly like-minded folks around you that have good intentions and a positive attitude. Just remember that there will always be someone that comes around to teach you the lesson you weren't aware that you even needed. This lesson can be good or not so good. Either way you must finish that lesson before you can move on 2 to the next one. Lessons are necessary regardless of what they are there to teach you about yourself.

Good luck and Peace to us all, and don't forget, enjoy your life and have fun with it every time you get the chance!

Thank you for reading **Common Sense** and if you feel that you already do and practice all of this, I will bet you that you know someone around you that could benefit from these thoughts. Please pass this book on to them but make sure that they really want it and won't just take it because you offered it and put it on a shelf. Once again; *"Knowledge not share is wasted"*

May you all live a long, spiritual, happy, loving, exciting, healthy, wealthy, (in whatever way you define wealth), wonderful life. I love you all and thank you for reading my thoughts. If you find value in them then please share it.

Signed,

A Concerned Human Being

ABOUT THE GLOBE ART

The globe and the symbols on it and what *I* am saying with them:

The first is the Earth, the wonderful planet that gives us life. It needs no explanation as it is what it is, our home.

2nd is the peace sign wrapped around it signifying the world peace that will benefit us all. The only reason that we don't have it is greed and a desire for power over others.

3rd is the two hearts in the middle because two hearts create twice as much love and also symbolizes the love we need for each other as human beings.

4th is the words Peace, Love and Respect. If we can create any two of them then that alone will create the 3rd. These are the things that will help to bring about world peace.

5th, the pineapple is universal welcome sign, 'nuff said.

6th is the palm tree and the crescent moon. The palm tree is one of the strongest trees to stand up to hurricanes and the moon has great influence over this planet, the tides and the inhabitants on it. The Palm and the Crescent are also on the SC flag.

7th is the Scales of Justice that stands for equal justice for all. In the scales is a woman and a man and this symbolizes the need for equal rights, pay, respect and treatment between the sexes for anything done at equal measure.

8th is the 11 finger MJ leaf. 11 is a mystical number and not that common on MJ plants and the leaf symbolizes both hemp and

MJ. Hemp is a sustainable resource that will help to save trees and make quality paper, clothing and many other things humans need. Almost anything made from a tree can be made from a hemp plant. Marijuana is a sustainable resource that has many healing and medicinal qualities that can help humans as well as a calming effect on most humans.

Last but not least is the shark fin that represents the dangers both large and small that we must all be aware of and respect at all times. For even a walk down the stairs can turn tragic if one is not sure of his footsteps. Likewise, as we walk through life, we need to be aware of our path and our surroundings as well as our fellow travelers. Even the best of intentions turn out other than planned. Be careful out there folks.

ACKNOWLEDGEMENT

I would like to thank everyone that helped me to edit my thoughts over the course of writing this book. I have never written a book before and their help with sentence structure, typos, chapter arrangement, better wording and many other areas have been priceless. It isn't perfect but neither am I. I am just sharing many things that have worked for me.

First I want to thank my Mother, Marian, for if it were not for her help in life then this book may have never happened. I miss you Mom and I love you.

I would like to thank Anthony Scolaro and his company, www.projectassistant.org for all their help with pulling the ideas for the artwork out of my head and refining them and creating the cover art work that you see. Special thanks go out to Isaac Bravo who is the artist of this wonderful cover. They also created the website, the store and the social media pages. I am forever grateful.

In no particular order I would like to thank; Zarah, Andrew, Noel, Tom, Robert, Marina, Mark, Don, Paul, Lita, Corky, Diana, Lisa and David as well as Byron whom suggested that I write this book while sharing this information with him. If I have left anyone out I apologize and thank you all.

ABOUT THE AUTHOR

Michael Goodyear

Michael Goodyear is a self-made man overflowing with hard-bought wisdom that he often downplays as common sense. An everyday hero that faces challenges with the ferocity of a lion and the patience of a Biblical Job. He is an inspiration to those who have worked under him and walked beside him.

A family man, entrepreneur, lifelong learner, and true friend who always leaves space for God and guidance to inform his decisions. It is with the utmost honor and respect that my words find a place alongside his in this work. Common Sense from this not so Common Man!

PRAISE FOR AUTHOR

Truly a collection of common sense and wisdom to inform our lives! A must-read for anyone looking to gain leverage and meaning in this grand human condition we call Life!

- ROBERT P. SOUTH AMERICA

Common Sense is a refreshing book on helping you help yourself while respecting others along the way. Written in a style that will feel as if you're having a conversation with the author.

- LISA N DAVID S.

"COMMON SENSE" is a guide to making a better "YOU". The earlier in life that you practice the lessons of this book the greater impact it will have on your life physically, mentally and financially.

- MARC A. FLA.

This book shares one man's Life experience and acquired logic in an Easy to read way. Every person of all age groups and backgrounds should read this book to understand life and gain sense of who we are as people and to handle life's challenges and show appreciation of its blessings. Wisdom shared is a timeless gift and common sense is the gift of wisdom.

- PAUL R. PA

If ONLY someone had told me...". Well, now someone HAS! That SOMEONE is Mickey Goodyear in his life-line reference "Common Sense". Drawing from his own experiences, he has thoughtfully addressed many common life challenges with practical guidance and recommendations that he would have welcomed during his critical adolescent years. This is a down-to-earth handbook addressing critical life SKILLS!. It contains immediate answers to everyday concerns with options and explanations that can provide long-term positive results.This handbook will be an invaluable companion for any young person; however, it was particularly written for preteens and young adults who have not had, or do not have, an involved parent or access to a mentor when issues arise. It is truly filled with that all-too elusive Common Sense which helps us to manage well this one and only life of ours.

- LITA M.

Made in the USA
Columbia, SC
20 December 2021

50989092R00104